Grillin' & Chili'n'

Grillin' & Chili'n'

More than Eighty Easy Recipes for Searing,
Sizzling, and Savoring Venison

KATE FIDUCCIA

The Lyons Press
Guilford, Connecticut
An imprint of The Globe Pequot Press

The Lyons Press is an imprint of The Globe Pequot Press.

10 9 8 7 6 5 4 3 2 1

Printed in China

Designed by LeAnna Weller Smith

Photographs on pages ii, xvii, xiii, xvi, 48, and 60 by Fiduccia Enterprises.

All other photographs by Liesa Cole.

ISBN 1-59228-169-9

Library of Congress Cataloging-in-Publication Data is available on file.

To my loves, supports, comrades, hunting partners,
and most helpful critics—my husband, Peter, and son, Cody.
I love you both.

Contents

Acknowledgments

There were many people who assisted me during the production of this book. I would like to thank Jeffrey Sohns from Sohns Appliances in Walden, New York, and Jim Reid at Coleman Company for their generous support of this project. Thanks also to Viking Kitchen Products; Valerie Gleason from Chef's Choice/EdgeCraft Corp.; Katie Mitchell from Bass Pro Shops; and Brad Moss from Totally Wild Seasonings.

Introduction

Why a venison cookbook on grilling and chili recipes? Having traveled the country hunting game and eating venison from coast to coast since the mid-eighties, I have found that these methods of preparing venison are two of the most popular ways in which to enjoy it. Many venison lovers grill and barbecue venison throughout the year as main meals for their families and guests. They relish a passion for the task and hardly call it a chore. In addition, many cooks know that a sure-fire meal that pleases all guests is venison chili. In fact, many of the outdoorsmen and women I speak with at sports shows tell me that the easiest way to cook their venison is in a ground state and the most frequently used and easily prepared recipe is one for chili. So, when it came time to put together a new cookbook on venison, it seemed to me that one combining grilling and chili recipes would be well-received by venison lovers everywhere.

Broadly defined, venison is any type of game meat. But, for the purposes of this cookbook, venison is defined as the more popular types of game meat: deer, elk, moose, and caribou. Whether you hunt for your own, receive venison from a friend, or order it through a retail outlet, the following recipes include the most-often prepared methods for steaks, ribs, burgers, sausages, and chili. I have also included a resource list of mail-order and Internet-order companies where you can obtain venison. You'll even find a facility that sells glatt kosher venison—mazel tav!

I begin with recipes for grilling steaks, ribs, chops, burgers, and sausages. No longer is cooking food over a hot fire simply a summertime option. Folks today grill year-round. There are grills built into kitchens, grills that are permanent built-in fixtures of patios, and the traditional gas and charcoal grills.

Following this section are popular, lip-smacking, belly-filling, breaking-a-sweat-or-two chilies. Not only will you find scrumptious chili recipes, there are also many recipes with chili as a main ingredient. Leftover chili is always delicious—oftentimes even better the next day—and I've included several recipes to give you a variety of ways to prepare a meal with it.

I love to read cookbooks and I'm sure you do, too. There are always a few pointers, tips, hints, or new information that I find while thumbing through them. But what I also like to see in a cookbook are suggestions or recipes for dishes to accompany the main recipes. So, in this volume, you will find just that—some of my own favorite side dishes, many of which can also be prepared on the grill.

The section on Marinades, Rubs, Butters, and Sauces is one to be taken lightly. *Literally.* I love the taste of venison and these recipes are suggested to merely highlight it or add a subtle flavor. To me, nothing destroys the exquisite taste of venison faster than a marinade that has completely altered its flavor.

It reminds me of sushi. Raw fish has a delicious taste all on its own. I prefer salmon, yellow tail tuna, and fatty tuna. I can eat sashimi as is—no soy sauce or wasabi. Every now and then, however, I dab on a little wasabi or dip a piece of fish in soy sauce to compliment the flavor of the fish. What I find odd is when someone takes a piece of raw fish and soaks it in soy sauce or slathers it with wasabi. Where's the taste of the fish? All that person is experiencing is a soy-soaked, wasabi-pasted, hot-tasting piece of something! So, with this in mind, to accentuate the flavor of venison, try the butter and sauce recipes as side accompaniments. Let a venison steak marinate for no more than an hour or so before grilling, dollop some Chile Butter on a burger when it's just hot off the grill or take a piece of sliced venison steak and dip a corner of it in some Creamy Blue Cheese Butter to enjoy the blend of the flavors.

I hope that you find some recipes to call your favorites and use them to please family and friends. Have fun with the venison recipes and enjoy some healthy eating, too!

GRILLS

What better way is there to unwind after a full day at the office than cooking outdoors with gentle breezes caressing your face that seem to wash away the stresses of the day?

Let's start with the grill. Whether it's a gas barbecue grill or a set-up of charcoal briquettes with a grilling grate on top, a fire is a fire. As long as the temperature is hot enough, you're good to go.

But which method should you use? There are pros and cons to both gas and charcoal. Gas grills fire up and heat up much more quickly than charcoal grills. They offer a strong heat source that is consistent and the temperature can be controlled as desired.

But for all this, there comes a higher price tag. A quality gas grill will have a drip pan that is easy to locate and empty, a gas gauge, sturdy legs, a thick metal grill grate, a built-in thermometer, and side burners for sauces and warming food.

Still there are those who swear by the taste that charcoal imparts to food. They also savor the special routine of setting up, lighting,

and tending a charcoal fire. There is an element of control as one pokes and prods at the coals to get the fire "just right." Another often sought-after benefit of charcoal grills is that they are easier to set up for wood smoking. With a kettle grill, you simply push aside the coals from the center, drop in the special wood (previously soaked in water), and wait for it to start smoking. An ideal charcoal grill will have a large grilling surface, an adjustable grate, an ash catcher, hinged grill grates, and a firebox. With a good charcoal grill, be sure there's enough room to set up a two-zone area for cooking: one hot and one not-so-hot area. For example, if you are cooking a steak with grilled onions, grill the onions in the section with the lower heat and cook the steak over the section with the higher heat.

Types of **gas** grills include those from Coleman, a company whose name is synonymous with the outdoors, which range from the 4000 to 9000i Grill. The 4000 stainless steel models offer a triple tent and chamber cooking system that virtually eliminates any hot or cold spots on the grill. The tent design also causes grease and drippings to drain away from the burner, which drastically reduces the chance of flare-ups. With 645 square inches of cooking space and 41,000 BTUs of grilling power, this unit packs a powerful punch.

Coleman's 9000i grill allows serious grillers to prepare an entire meal in one spot. With a unique wraparound look, this unit has four burners and three different cooking areas. Each of the cooking areas has its own hood. With 512 square inches of primary cooking space and 373 square inches of warming space, the center zone and the two side zones generate a total output of 42,000 BTUs. This grill offers pivoting upper shelves that also serve as warming units. This is one of my all-time favorite grills.

Weber's Summit series continues with quality grills with attractive features. The Summit Gold A has a total cooking area of 902 square inches with a total power output of 57,600 BTUs. It also includes a warming rack and a warm-up basket area.

Viking has a 53-inch portable gas grill with an integrated side burner and electronic ignition. This exceptional unit has 836 square inches of grilling space and boasts a combined main burner output of 75,000 BTUs. It also has an infrared rotisserie system, a removable smoker tray for wood chips or chunks, and an extra deep sealed burner box for easier temperature maintenance.

Char-Broil's Charcoal/Gas Grill is a combination of the two fuel sources, offering the speedy convenience of propane and the tasty flavor of charcoal. A charcoal tray allows the grill's propane burners to ignite the charcoal and then uses the burning coals to cook. When you're done cooking, just lift out the charcoal pan when it has cooled and dump the charcoal.

Types of **charcoal grills** include Weber's One-Touch Platinum charcoal grill. The surface cooking area is 18½ inches in diameter and the kettle is vented on the top and base to adjust for wind and aerate hot zones for perfect grilling. This grill also features a one-touch cleaning system.

Coleman's new series of RoadTrip grills include the RoadTrip Charcoal Grill with 385 square inches of total grilling surface. This handy and easy-to-set-up grill includes a "Quick Cool" ash collection system, easy-glide wheels, and a detachable shelf. It comes standard with one grill and one griddle cooking surface.

Char-Broil's CB940 series heavy-duty, four-wheeled grills are made of steel with cast-iron cooking grates. These grills have 533 square inches of cooking space, two side shelves, a lower storage rack, and an adjustable-height charcoal grate.

These are a few of the types of gas and charcoal grills available. Other variations include the hibachi, kettle grill, table grill, and smoker.

TOOLS TO GET THE JOB DONE
Here are some essential tools to help make grilling more enjoyable:

- *Long-handled tongs:* To turn food or poke the fire. This tool should be made with metal strong enough to pick up a large piece of food without buckling. The tongs should also be long enough so that you do not burn your hand when turning food with them.

- *Long metal spatula:* To turn foods, especially delicate foods such as burgers and steaks. It is also great to loosen foods that have become stuck to the grill.

- *Hinged grill rack or basket:* Ideal for cooking delicate items such as venison burgers or vegetables. The rack will hold the food items together so they don't fall through the grill grate. Make sure the grilling basket has a long heatproof handle to make turning easier and safer.

- *Instant read thermometer:* Very important to accurately gauge the temperature of meat.

- *Flat metal or round bamboo skewers:* Necessary for tasty shish kebobs. The flat metal skewers help prevent food from spinning around as you turn it to cook.

- *Basting brush with a long handle and natural bristles:* The handle should be long enough so you don't burn your hand or arm when basting food. The bristles should be natural because the synthetic bristles will burn over the fire.

- *Stiff wire brush for cleaning the grill:* A clean grill is a good grill. Keep the wire brush handy for cleaning after every cooking session. Again, be sure that the handle is long enough so that you don't burn your hand or arm when cleaning the grill.

Grills and grilling accessories run the gamut from economy to deluxe, and you can find them in all types of stores from Wal-Mart, Home Depot, and Sears to specialty kitchen and home centers across the nation. So, get out your grill, fire it up, and let's get cooking!

CHAPTER ONE

Grillin'

STEAKS, RIBS & CHOPS

BURGERS

SAUSAGES

Grilling is synonymous with no fuss, more flavor, and lots of fun. Parties where food is cooked on the grill seem to garner great enthusiasm and promote commingling, as the grilled food items become the topic of conversation.

Throwing some venison on the grill will not only heighten anticipation and lower fat intake, it will also heighten the level of cuisine. The following recipes are simple and delicious. Have fun and enjoy!

Balsamic Buck Steaks

SERVES: 3

PREP TIME: 5 MINUTES

MARINATING TIME: 1 TO 2 HOURS

COOKING TIME: 10 MINUTES

⅔ cup balsamic vinegar

½ cup olive oil

½ teaspoon thyme

4 garlic cloves, chopped

3 venison loin steaks, 6 to 8 ounces each, trimmed of all fat and connective tissue

sea salt, to taste

freshly ground black pepper, to taste

This recipe was tested with a buck that came from our new farm in upstate New York. It was our first hunting season there, and the preceding weekend hit us hard with a three-foot snowfall. The weight of the snow and ice knocked down trees and we lost power for four days. But that didn't stop the hardiest of hunters, including yours truly, from taking a buck (and a tasty one at that) on opening day.

Combine the vinegar, olive oil, thyme, and garlic cloves in a non-metallic container. Place the venison steaks in a glass dish or plastic bag and pour the marinade over the steaks. Refrigerate for 1 to 2 hours, turning occasionally to evenly marinate the steaks.

Preheat the grill for about 20 minutes. The grill should be hot enough that you can hold your hand over it for only a few seconds.

While the grill is heating up, remove the steaks from the refrigerator to let them come to room temperature. Drain the steaks, blot them dry, and reserve the strained marinade. Place the marinade in a small saucepan and heat it over high heat. Let it boil down to a thicker consistency.

Place the steaks on the grill and cook for about 2 to 3 minutes each side, depending upon the thickness of the steaks. During the last few minutes of cooking, season with salt and pepper and brush some of the glaze on the steaks. Serve immediately.

Trimming Meat

Venison fat is not very tasty. Unlike beef or pork fat, venison fat is bitter and can often impart its flavor into the meat if it is not trimmed off prior to being prepared. Remove all sinew, gristle, silverskin, and fat. Remember that grilling is a dry-cooking method and as such, the heat tends to dry out the meat. Since venison has very little fat to begin with, it must be either cooked very quickly or basted while on the grill. Basting will help keep the meat moist and succulent.

Wasabi Grilled Elk Steak

Our household is filled with sushi lovers. Part of the enjoyment of eating sushi is experiencing the pain/pleasure of wasabi. With just a dab, one experiences the slight "hotness" with the fish. Glop a bit more on and you can get that "It-hurts-so-good!" feeling along with red, watery eyes and a runny nose!

The proportions of the ingredients in the wasabi butter below are just right to offer an exquisite flavor to the elk steaks. But, if you enjoy eating "the hotter the butter the better," then adjust the amount of wasabi as you like.

Preheat the grill for about 20 minutes. The grill should be hot enough that you can hold your hand over it for only a few seconds.

Cream the butter with a fork and then add the wasabi, ginger, and soy sauce.

When the grill is ready, grill each steak about 3 to 4 minutes each side (depending upon the thickness of the steaks). As the steaks cook, season lightly with salt and pepper. Once steaks are done (I suggest cooking them no more than medium-rare), remove to serving platters, spread the butter on each steak, and cut each steak in half. Serve immediately.

SERVES: 4

PREP TIME: 15 MINUTES

COOKING TIME: 10 MINUTES

½ cup unsalted butter

1 teaspoon prepared wasabi

1 teaspoon fresh ginger, finely minced

1 teaspoon dark soy sauce

salt and pepper, to taste

2 large elk steaks, about ¾ pound each, trimmed of all fat and connective tissue

Cuban Grilled Venison

SERVES: 4 TO 6

PREP TIME: 10 MINUTES

MARINATING TIME: 1 HOUR

COOKING TIME: 10 MINUTES

8 venison steaks, 4 to 6 ounces each, ½ inch thick, trimmed of all fat and connective tissue

8 limes or lemons

5 garlic cloves, crushed

1 tablespoon crushed red pepper flakes

3 tablespoons olive oil

salt and pepper, to taste

unsalted butter

On a trip to southern Florida, I first tasted meat prepared Cuban style and have since created this recipe for venison. The unique blend of citrus, garlic, and red pepper is truly delicious with venison—especially when it's grilled.

Preheat the grill for about 20 minutes. The grill should be hot enough that you can hold your hand over it for only a few seconds.

Flatten the steaks with a butcher hammer until uniform in thickness. Rub the garlic cloves into the steaks, leaving a little bit of garlic on each piece of meat. Salt each steak lightly. Cut the limes or lemons in half. Squeeze the juice over each piece of meat as you stack it in a glass or plastic bowl. Marinate for 1 hour.

Brush each piece of meat with oil and season lightly with red pepper flakes just before cooking over a hot fire. Grill about 2 to 3 minutes on each side. Do not grill them more than medium-rare. Season and butter. Serve hot.

Savory Grilled Venison

The rich, full taste and slight saltiness of a good blue cheese makes a savory topping for venison steaks hot off the grill. Enjoy this with a fine white Burgundy.

Preheat the grill for about 20 minutes. The grill should be hot enough that you can hold your hand over it for only a few seconds.

In a small saucepan over medium heat, heat the butter until it foams. Add the shallots and cook until soft. Add the vinegar, stir, and cook until the vinegar is evaporated, about 2 minutes. Turn the heat to low and stir in the blue cheese and cayenne pepper. Stir and adjust the seasoning as necessary. Keep warm while the steaks are grilling.

Season the steaks with pepper. Grill about 3 to 4 minutes each side, depending upon the thickness of the steaks. It is best to cook the steaks to medium-rare. Once done, remove the steaks to serving platters and spread the cheese mixture on top. Garnish with the minced chives and serve immediately.

SERVES 4

PREP TIME: 15 MINUTES

COOKING TIME: 10 MINUTES

1 tablespoon unsalted butter

¼ cup shallots, minced

2 tablespoons white wine vinegar

6 ounces blue cheese, crumbled

cayenne pepper, to taste

2 pounds venison steaks, trimmed of all fat and connective tissue

¼ cup garlic chives, minced

pepper, to taste

20 Gauge Caribou Steaks

SERVES: 4 TO 5
PREP TIME: 10 MINUTES
COOKING TIME: 10 MINUTES

4 caribou steaks, about 8 to 10 ounces each, trimmed of all fat and connective tissue

1 cup Myron's 20 Gauge Sauce

2 tablespoons olive oil

2 large onions, cut into ½-inch thick slices

Note: Myron's 20 Gauge Sauce is an all-natural sauce that is perfect for both fish and game. It is a savory blend of soy sauce, red wine, natural brown sugars, fresh garlic, olive oil, rice vinegar, and Myron's secret blend of seasonings. Additional information can be found in the listing of sources at the end of the book.

I met Myron many moons ago when he gave a cooking demo at a sports show where my husband, Peter, was also giving deer hunting seminars. Both Myron and his sauces are unique. We tasted his 20 Gauge Sauce on grilled chicken and have been blessed with flavorsome grilled meats, fish, and poultry ever since. This is one of our fast 'n' easy favorites.

Preheat the grill for about 20 minutes. The grill should be hot enough that you can hold your hand over it for only a few seconds.

While the grill is heating, place the venison steaks in a non-reactive dish and pour about ½ cup of the sauce on the steaks. Turn the steaks to coat well.

When the grill is ready, oil the grill grate and place the steaks on the grill. While they cook, baste them with the remaining ½ cup of sauce. Cook about 3 to 5 minutes per side, depending upon the thickness of the venison.

Place the onions on the grill and lightly baste with the 20 Gauge Sauce. Turn after 3 to 4 minutes and baste again.

When the steaks are done, place on a platter and let sit for a few minutes. Serve with the grilled onions on the side.

Scallion Grilled Steak

This grilled steak dish has some of the flavors from many of the popular Korean dishes prepared today. The piquant aroma that wafts from the grill certainly revs up one's appetite while the steaks cook!

In a nonmetallic bowl, mix together the sesame seeds, soy sauce, sake, scallions, garlic cloves, sesame oil, ginger, sugar, and black pepper. Place the venison steaks in a glass baking pan and pour the marinade over the venison. Refrigerate for 1 hour, turning occasionally to evenly marinate the steaks.

Preheat the grill for about 20 minutes. The grill should be hot enough that you can hold your hand over it for only a few seconds.

Remove the venison steaks from the marinade and pat dry. Bring the steaks to room temperature before grilling. Place the steaks on the grill and cook for about 3 to 5 minutes each side, until medium-rare. Baste occasionally with the marinade. Serve hot.

SERVES: 4

PREP TIME: 10 MINUTES

MARINATING TIME: 1 HOUR

COOKING TIME: 10 MINUTES

1 tablespoon sesame seeds, toasted

4 tablespoons soy sauce

2 tablespoons sake

5 scallions, sliced

4 garlic cloves, peeled and minced

1½ tablespoons sesame oil

1 tablespoon fresh ginger, shredded

2 teaspoons sugar

freshly ground black pepper, to taste

4 venison steaks, 6 ounces each, trimmed of all fat and connective tissue

Note: To toast the sesame seeds, place them in a small skillet over medium heat for about 1 minute, shaking the pan as they cook to brown them lightly on all sides.

Garlic-Lime Venison Steak

SERVES: 4

PREP TIME: 15 MINUTES

COOKING TIME: 10 MINUTES

4 venison steaks, 6 to 8 ounces
   each, trimmed of all fat and
   connective tissue

1 pound portobello mushrooms,
   sliced ¼ inch thick

2 tablespoons olive oil

salt, to taste

pepper, to taste

Garlic-Lime Rub (see page 157)

Sylvia, a college friend of mine, was from Cuba and loved to share with me some of her native recipes during the seemingly endless winter months in upstate New York. I later adapted this flavorful one for venison.

Place the venison steaks in a glass baking dish and, with a pastry brush, lightly coat both sides of the steaks with the Garlic-Lime Rub. Let sit for 15 to 20 minutes.

While the steaks sit, preheat the grill for about 20 minutes. The grill should be hot enough that you can hold your hand over it for only a few seconds.

Place the mushrooms in a bowl and drizzle with olive oil and a little salt. Toss to coat. Place the mushrooms in an oiled, long-handled, hinged, grill basket. Set on the grill to cook in a cooler section of the grill.

Place the steaks in the center of the grill. Grill about 2 minutes each side, while basting with the rub. Grill the mushrooms about 2 to 3 minutes per side and season with salt and pepper.

Transfer the steaks to plates and let sit for a few minutes. Serve with the grilled mushrooms on the side.

To Cover or Not to Cover?

When should you cover or not cover a grill? When a small or thin cut of food requires a quick grilling time, then I usually don't cover it. When I cook thin steaks, cutlets, and even some vegetables that require only a few minutes on each side, I also leave the grill uncovered. With thicker cuts, however, I usually sear the meat first over high heat, and then either lower the heat or place the meat on a cooler section of the grill and close the lid. When the grill is covered, it turns it into an oven of sorts.

Extra-Virgin Moose Steaks

If you relish the flavor of quality extra-virgin olive oil, then you will love this recipe. The extra-virgin olive oil imparts its own unique depth of flavor to the moose steaks.

Preheat the grill for about 20 minutes. The grill should be hot enough that you can hold your hand over it for only a few seconds. When the grill is ready, oil the grill plate.

Place the steaks on the hot grill and cook 5 to 7 minutes each side. Season with salt and pepper while on the grill. While the steak is cooking the last minute or so, carefully drizzle a little olive oil on the top of the steaks. Be careful of any flare-ups from the grill. Remove with tongs and set on a platter, drizzle the remaining oil on the steaks and let them sit for a few minutes to let the juices set evenly throughout the meat. Cut the steaks in half and plate them with olives as a garnish.

Serve with marinated fresh mozzarella and tomatoes on the side.

SERVES: 4

PREP TIME: 5 MINUTES

COOKING TIME: 15 MINUTES

2 moose sirloin steaks, about 1 pound each, at least 1 inch thick, trimmed of all fat and connective tissue

kosher salt, to taste

black pepper, to taste

¾ cup extra-virgin olive oil

16 green olives, sliced in half lengthwise, for garnish

Korean-Style Grilled Venison

SERVES: 4

PREP TIME: 15 MINUTES

MARINATING TIME: 45 MINUTES

COOKING TIME: 10 MINUTES

Marinade:

4 scallions, coarsely chopped

3 large cloves garlic, finely chopped

1 teaspoon ginger, finely chopped

3 tablespoons soy sauce

2 tablespoons sugar

2 tablespoons cold water

1 tablespoon sesame oil

2 tablespoons toasted sesame seeds, crushed

2 teaspoons mirin (rice wine) or dry white wine

freshly ground black pepper, to taste

1½ pounds venison tenderloin or sirloin steak, trimmed of all fat and connective tissue

1 tablespoon vegetable oil (approximate)

This recipe is absolutely delicious when grilled over an open fire. It can also be prepared in a wok when you can't grill.

In a 2-cup glass measuring cup, or other non-reactive container, combine all the marinade ingredients; stir well. Slice the venison across the grain into ¼-inch thick slices. (If time permits, place the venison in the freezer for about 45 minutes to firm up the meat. It will make cutting thin slices easier.)

Place the venison strips in a shallow glass baking dish. Pour the marinade over the venison. Stir to thoroughly coat the strips. Cover with plastic wrap and refrigerate for about 45 minutes to 1 hour.

Remove the venison from the refrigerator and bring to room temperature before grilling.

Preheat the grill for about 20 minutes. The grill should be hot enough that you can hold your hand over it for only a few seconds. Lightly oil the grill rack. Cook the venison in batches until the strips are seared on the outside, but still rare in the inside, not more than 1 minute per side.

Serve hot with Grilled Mushrooms & Onions (see page 126).

Zesty Elk Steaks

If you like pepper, you'll love this recipe with tri-color peppercorns. Don't worry if black peppercorns are all you have, they will work well, too.

SERVES: 4

PREP TIME: 10 MINUTES

MARINATING TIME: 30 MINUTES

COOKING TIME: 10 MINUTES

Combine all rub ingredients in a mortar and grind with a pestle. Rub the steaks on both sides with the peppercorn mixture, pressing the peppercorns into the flesh of the meat. Let the steaks sit for about 30 minutes.

Preheat the grill for about 20 minutes. The grill should be hot enough that you can hold your hand over it for only a few seconds.

Lightly oil the grill rack. Place the steaks on the hot grill and let cook about 3 minutes each side, depending upon the thickness of the steaks. Turn the steaks with a set of tongs, not a fork. When cooked to medium-rare, remove the steaks from the grill and let them sit for 2 minutes to let the juices set evenly. Top each steak with some of the garlic butter and serve immediately.

Peppercorn Rub:

3 tablespoons whole black peppercorns

3 tablespoons whole white peppercorns

3 tablespoons whole pink peppercorns

1 tablespoon mustard seed

2 teaspoons garlic powder

1½ teaspoons kosher salt

4 venison steaks, 6 to 8 ounces each, trimmed of all fat and connective tissue.

1 tablespoon olive oil, as needed

4 tablespoons Garlic Butter (see page 155)

Smoky Grilled Venison Sirloin

SERVES: 6

PREP TIME: 10 MINUTES

MARINATING TIME: 1 TO 2 HOURS

COOKING TIME: 8 MINUTES

6 sirloin venison steaks,
about 8 to 10 ounces each

¼ cup canola oil

1 cup Smoky Marinade
(see page 150)

I enjoy the unique aromas and flavors that different types of wood impart to foods that are cooked over them. Some of my favorites are hickory, mesquite, and apple. There are times, however, when cooking with wood is not practical. The marinade created for this recipe uses liquid smoke, which does a good job of mimicking that smoky flavor.

Marinate the steaks in the Smoky Marinade for 1 to 2 hours.

Preheat the grill for about 20 minutes. The grill should be hot enough that you can hold your hand over it for only a few seconds.

Remove the steaks from the marinade. Lightly oil the grill plate. Place the steaks on the grill and let cook until medium-rare, about 4 minutes each side.

Simple Smoke

You don't have to burn whole logs of mesquite to get its customary rich, smoky aroma and flavor. Wood chips will do fine. Soak the chips (mesquite, cherry, apple, hickory, alder, or oak) in water for about an hour. Make sure the water covers them completely. When soaked through, drain the wood chips and then toss them onto the hot coals.

Citrus Grilled Venison

In Texas many years ago, my husband, Peter, and I had returned from a mid-day's hunt for quail when we enjoyed grilled venison steaks for early supper. The hint of the marinade was utterly delicious. While the camp chef (aka creator of the recipe) shared some of the ingredients with me, getting all of the ingredients was a nut I could not crack! I have, however, developed this recipe that blends the tangy, sweet, and salty flavors that satiates all who try it.

SERVES: 4 TO 6
PREP TIME: 10 MINUTES
MARINATING TIME: 1 TO 2 HOURS
COOKING TIME: 10 MINUTES

In a small saucepan over medium heat, place the orange juice and honey. Stir until the honey is completely dissolved. Remove from heat and add the lemon juice, sesame oil, soy sauce, and Worcestershire sauce.

When cooled, pour the marinade over the steaks. Cover and marinate in the refrigerator 1 to 2 hours.

Preheat the grill for about 20 minutes. The grill should be hot enough that you can hold your hand over it for only a few seconds.

Remove the steaks from the marinade and bring to room temperature. Pat the steaks dry. Lightly oil the grill. Place the steaks on the grill and cook about 3 to 5 minutes per side. Do not let them cook beyond medium-rare.

Remove from the grill and let sit to let the juices set. Serve immediately.

1 cup orange juice

¼ cup honey

¼ cup lemon juice

2 tablespoons sesame oil

1 tablespoon soy sauce

¼ cup Worcestershire sauce

6 venison steaks, ¾ inch thick each

"Aye—There's the Rub" Grilled Venison Steaks

SERVES: 6

PREP TIME: 10 MINUTES

COOKING TIME: 6 MINUTES

Dry rubs create a nice crunchy crust on the steaks. This one always has everyone asking for more!

6 boneless venison steaks, about 6 ounces each, trimmed of all fat and connective tissue

2 tablespoons canola oil

1 cup "Aye—There the Rub" Rub (see page 158)

Press the rub into the steaks on both sides, to coat the steaks well. Set aside.

Preheat the grill for about 20 minutes. The grill should be hot enough that you can hold your hand over it for only a few seconds.

Oil the grill grate before placing the rubbed steaks on the grill. Place the steaks on the grill and cook for about 2 to 3 minutes each side. Cook only to medium-rare, not any longer. Remove from grill and let sit for about 3 minutes to allow the juices to set. Serve hot with Grilled Eggplant & Smoked Mozzarella (see page 134).

Barbecued Caribou Chops

This is one of my favorite recipes for either caribou or moose meat. The marinade accentuates the delicate flavor of the venison and the high-heat cooking method heightens the combination of the two.

Place the chops in a shallow glass baking dish. In a small bowl, mix together the olive oil, onion, pepper, parsley, paprika, salt, wine, and lemon juice. Mix well. Pour over the chops and turn the chops to coat well. Marinate in the refrigerator for about 1 to 2 hours, turning occasionally.

Preheat the grill for about 20 minutes. The grill should be hot enough that you can hold your hand over it for only a few seconds.

Remove the chops from the marinade and bring to room temperature. Blot dry before placing them on the grill. Lightly oil the grill plate and set the chops on the grill. Grill for about 2 to 3 minutes per side, being careful to cook them no more than medium-rare.

Serve immediately.

SERVES: 4

PREP TIME: 10 MINUTES

MARINATING TIME: 1 TO 2 HOURS

COOKING TIME: 6 MINUTES

4 caribou loin chops, trimmed of all fat and connective tissue

¼ cup olive oil

1 small onion, chopped

1 tablespoon freshly ground pepper

1 tablespoon fresh parsley, chopped

⅛ teaspoon paprika

½ teaspoon sea salt

¼ red wine (Merlot or Cabernet will do fine)

3 tablespoons lemon juice

canola oil, as needed for the grill

Grilled Venison Wellington

SERVES: 4

PREP TIME: 20 MINUTES

COOKING TIME: 20 MINUTES

4 venison loin medallions, about 1½ inches thick, trimmed of all fat and connective tissue

2 tablespoons olive oil

salt and freshly ground black pepper, to taste

4 large portobello mushroom caps

4 large slices Italian bread, ½ inch thick

3 cups Brown (Is Down) Sauce (see page 159)

⅓ cup duck liver pate, room temperature

In my first venison cookbook, I shared my recipe for the traditional Venison Wellington that's baked in the oven. This twist on that classic is one of my fancier preparations for the grill. It's sure to please all your guests.

Preheat the grill for about 20 minutes. The grill should be hot enough that you can hold your hand over it for only a few seconds.

Brush the medallions and portobellos with the oil and season with salt and pepper.

Lightly oil the grill plate before placing the medallions on the grill. Cook over high heat until they are seared on both sides (1 to 2 minutes). Cook until the internal temperature is 125° F (medium-rare). Remove from the grill and let them sit for 5 minutes to let the juices set.

Grill the mushrooms until seared on both sides. Set aside and keep warm.

On a cooler section of the grill, lightly toast the Italian bread slices on both sides.

Heat the brown sauce in a small saucepan. Spread about 1 tablespoon of the pate on each slice of toasted bread. Slice the mushrooms and arrange them on top of the pate. Slice the medallions into ¼-inch thick strips and layer them on top of the mushroom slices.

Drizzle the brown sauce across the venison and serve warm.

Portobello Caribou Loin

Portobello mushroom caps are deliciously meaty. Seasoned with salt, pepper, and a little balsamic vinegar, they can be a meal on their own. My recipe for these mushrooms can be prepared on the grill or even under a broiler.

In a small glass bowl place the mushrooms in 2 tablespoons oil, with 4 garlic cloves, 1 tablespoon lemon juice, and salt and pepper to taste. Set aside. In a shallow glass baking dish, place the venison loin. In a small bowl, combine 2 tablespoons oil, 4 garlic cloves, 1 tablespoon lemon juice, thyme, red wine, salt and pepper. Stir to combine. Pour over the loin and turn the loin to coat it well. Set aside for 20 minutes.

Preheat the grill for about 20 minutes. The grill should be hot enough that you can hold your hand over it for only a few seconds.

Remove the loin from the marinade and place it on the grill. Let it cook and turn about every 5 minutes, until the internal temperature is about 125°F (medium-rare). Remove from the grill and let sit to allow the juices to set evenly throughout the meat.

While the loin is resting, remove the portobello mushrooms from the marinade. Place on the grill for about 3 to 5 minutes each side. When done, slice the mushrooms and plate with each steak. Each steak can be served with a dollop of Shallot-Lemon Butter (see page 152).

SERVES: 4

PREP TIME: 10 MINUTES

MARINATING TIME: 20 MINUTES

COOKING TIME: 20 MINUTES

4 portobello mushroom caps

4 tablespoons canola oil (2 and 2)

8 large garlic cloves, minced (4 and 4)

2 tablespoons lemon juice (1 and 1)

salt and freshly ground pepper, to taste

½ teaspoon dried thyme

3 tablespoons red wine (a Cabernet will do well)

2½ pounds caribou loin, trimmed of all fat and connective tissue

Sesame Venison Medallions

SERVES: 6 TO 8

PREP TIME: 10 MINUTES

MARINATING TIME: 1 TO 2 HOURS

COOKING TIME: 5 MINUTES

¼ cup canola oil

¼ cup blended sesame oil

¼ cup soy sauce

2 tablespoons fresh lemon juice

2 tablespoons fresh ginger, grated

1½ to 2 pounds venison loin, cut into medallions about ½ inch to ¾ inch thick

2 tablespoons sesame seeds

Blended sesame oil combines the odorless pale yellow sesame oil that is often used for frying with the dark brown Chinese sesame oil that has a strong nutty taste. The combination is excellent, especially when used in a marinade as in this recipe.

In a small nonmetallic bowl, whisk together the oils, soy sauce, lemon juice, and ginger. Place the venison medallions in a shallow glass baking dish. Pour the marinade over the medallions. Turn to coat completely. Cover the dish with plastic wrap and refrigerate for 1 to 2 hours.

Remove the medallions from the refrigerator and bring to room temperature.

Preheat the grill for about 20 minutes. The grill should be hot enough that you can hold your hand over it for only a few seconds.

Remove the medallions from the marinade and pat dry. The leftover marinade can be placed in a small saucepan, boiled, and then used as a baste if desired.

Lightly oil the grill plate. Place the medallions on the grill and let cook 2 to 3 minutes each side. Do not cook more than medium-rare. Remove the medallions and set aside for 5 minutes for the juices to set.

In a small skillet over medium heat, place the sesame seeds. Let the seeds cook to a light golden-brown color. Shake the pan occasionally to move the seeds around. Remove them from the heat and sprinkle on the medallions. Serve the medallions immediately. They can be served with Corn 'n' Pepper Summer Salad (see page 145).

Keeping Grill Tools Neat and Tidy

One of my pet peeves is cleaning the grill tools after each and every use. While I hang my tools next to the grill when I am cooking, I store them in the kitchen when they are not in use. To avoid a mess with the grill brush/scraper, I place the head in a small zip-lock bag and close the top around the handle. This way, I don't have to clean the brush after each use, but my drawers stay grit-free.

Molasses Grilled Venison Tenderloin

I was on a remote horse pack trip in beautiful southwest Colorado when the cook prepared a grilled dinner using a deliciously unique molasses marinade. Over the years, I have developed my own version that I'm sure you will enjoy, too.

SERVES: 6

PREP TIME: 10 MINUTES

MARINATING TIME: 1 HOUR

COOKING TIME: 20 MINUTES

Marinate the tenderloin in the Zesty Molasses Marinade for 30 minutes to 1 hour.

Preheat the grill for about 20 minutes. The grill should be hot enough that you can hold your hand over it for only a few seconds.

Cook the tenderloin on the grill for about 15 to 20 minutes, depending upon its thickness. Turn every 5 minutes or so. Do not let it cook past medium-rare (125° to 130°F). Remove from grill and let rest for about 5 minutes to let the juices settle. Slice and serve immediately. Serve with Grilled Potatoes and Crunchy Grilled Garlic Bread (see pages 142 and 137).

1½ pounds venison tenderloin, trimmed of all fat and connective tissue

½ cup Zesty Molasses Marinade (see page 151)

Spicy Venison Shish Kebobs

SERVES: 4

PREP TIME: 20 MINUTES

MARINATING TIME: 1 HOUR

COOKING TIME: 10 MINUTES

1½ pounds venison tenderloin, cut into 1-inch chunks, trimmed of all fat and connective tissue

4 cloves garlic, minced

1 teaspoon salt

1 teaspoon ground cumin

1 teaspoon freshly ground black pepper

1 teaspoon cayenne pepper

4 tablespoons canola oil

1 red tomato, seeded and cut into 1-inch chunks

1 green bell pepper, seeded and cut into 1-inch chunks

1 onion, peeled and cut into 1-inch chunks

10 small red-skinned new potatoes, skin on, cooked

4 long metal skewers or 8 bamboo skewers soaked in cold water for 1 hour

salt and pepper, to taste

This classic shish kebob recipe spices up the venison a bit. The accompanying vegetables and potatoes complement it nicely.

In a bowl, combine the venison, garlic, salt, cumin, black pepper, cayenne pepper, and oil. Stir to combine well and thoroughly coat the venison chunks. Cover and marinate in the refrigerator for 1 hour.

Preheat the grill for about 20 minutes. The grill should be hot enough that you can hold your hand over it for only a few seconds.

Remove the venison chunks from the marinade and thread them onto the skewers, alternating the tomatoes, peppers, onions, and potatoes. Place on the grill and turn every 2 minutes, until the venison is cooked to medium-rare (about 8 to 10 minutes). Season with salt and pepper to taste. Remove from grill, unthread from skewers, and serve immediately.

Be Careful with that Marinade!
Never put meat back into the same
pan that contained the marinade.
Bacteria from the meat may remain in
the juices. Always put the cooked
meat in a clean dish.

Teriyaki Onion & Venison Ribbons

Asian-style cooking has gained tremendous popularity through-out the world in recent years. It's not uncommon to find Chinese, Japanese, Korean, or even Thai restaurants in many suburban and rural communities today. In fact, one of the more well-known Asian condiments, teriyaki sauce, can be found on restaurant, cafeteria, school, and institutional menus. Teriyaki has great appeal among those who like to grill both meats and fish, too. One of our favorite ways to grill salmon steaks is with a teriyaki glaze. This recipe is suitable for beef as well.

Preheat the grill for about 20 minutes. The grill should be hot enough that you can hold your hand over it for only a few seconds.

Combine the soy sauce, sugar, sake, and garlic cloves in a nonmetallic container. The venison should be at room temperature. Thread the venison and onion onto the skewers. Reserve some of the sauce for dipping after the venison is grilled.

Place the skewers on the grill for about 30 seconds. Baste and turn again. Continue basting and turning until the venison is medium-rare. Remember that some carry-over heat will continue to cook the venison after you remove it from the grill. Serve the venison and onions hot with the dipping sauce set aside earlier.

SERVES: 4

PREP TIME: 5 MINUTES

COOKING TIME: 5 MINUTES

¼ cup regular soy sauce

¼ cup plus 1 tablespoon sugar

1 tablespoon sake

2 garlic cloves, minced

1 pound venison loin, sliced across the grain into ¼-inch thick strips, trimmed of all fat and connective tissue

1 medium red onion, cut into 1-inch square chunks

8 bamboo skewers soaked in cold water for 30 minutes

Note: If you are preparing this from a large piece of loin (such as moose, elk, or caribou), you can fold over each loin strip to pierce it twice or you can also place the threaded skewers in an oiled, hinged grill basket to help distribute the weight of the venison.

Tequila Elk Fajitas

SERVES: 6 TO 8

PREP TIME: 20 MINUTES

MARINATING TIME: 1 TO 2 HOURS

COOKING TIME: 15 TO 20 MINUTES

2 pounds elk skirt or flank steak, trimmed of all fat and connective tissue

½ cup tequila

¼ cup fresh lime juice

2 tablespoons canola oil

3 garlic cloves, minced

1 teaspoon ground cumin

1 teaspoon dried oregano, crumbled

½ teaspoon freshly ground pepper

½ teaspoon red pepper flakes

2 tablespoons canola oil

2 large red onions, cut crosswise into ½-inch thick slices

3 large green bell peppers, seeded and cut crosswise into thick rings

salt and pepper, to taste

12 flour tortillas, 10 inches in diameter

salsa, guacamole, and/or sour cream as accompaniments

I like to prepare this recipe for an informal gathering or a week-night family meal.

Place the elk steak in a shallow glass baking dish. Combine the tequila, lime juice, canola oil, garlic, cumin, oregano, and peppers in a small glass bowl. Whisk to combine. Pour the marinade over the elk steak and turn to coat thoroughly. Cover and refrigerate for 1 to 2 hours.

Preheat the grill for about 20 minutes. The grill should be hot enough that you can hold your hand over it for only a few seconds.

Brush the grill rack with oil and place the onion and pepper rings on the grill. Grill for 2 to 3 minutes each side. Season with salt and pepper. Set aside and keep warm while the elk steak cooks.

Remove the elk steak from the marinade and pat it dry. Brush the grill rack with oil before placing the steak on the grill. Grill for about 8 to 10 minutes. Turn every 2 to 3 minutes and baste with the remaining marinade.

When done, remove the steak from the grill and let it sit 5 minutes to allow the juices to settle evenly. While it is sitting, warm up the tortillas on the grill. With a pair of tongs, place

one tortilla at a time on the grill and turn after 10 seconds, depending how hot the grill is. Let it cook on the other side no more than 5 seconds and place it back on a platter. Repeat the process for the remaining tortillas.

Slice the steak on a diagonal, and place a few slices of elk steak and some pepper and onion rings on each warmed tortilla. Top with additional accompaniments as desired, fold in the sides, roll up tightly, and eat out of hand.

Boursin Blackened Venison Quesadillas

This is one of my favorite spicy recipes that is rich and satisfying. Boursin is a savory triple cream cheese flavored with garlic and herbs. Serve this with a chilled Sauvignon Blanc.

SERVES: 4

PREP TIME: 5 MINUTES

MARINATING TIME: 30 MINUTES

COOKING TIME: 12 MINUTES

Sprinkle the venison steak with the Crazy Cajun seasoning and let it sit at room temperature for about 30 minutes.

Preheat the grill for about 20 minutes. The grill should be hot enough that you can hold your hand over it for only a few seconds.

Place the steaks on the grill and cook for about 3 to 5 minutes each side, depending upon the size of the steaks. Remove when the steaks are medium-rare. Cut into slices and set aside.

Spread the Boursin cheese on each of the tortillas. Place venison steak strips across half of the tortilla and fold over the other half. Place the tortilla on the grill and heat for about 30 seconds each side.

Serve immediately. Some side accompaniments may include sour cream, salsa, guacamole, chopped black olives, or sliced jalapenos.

1 to 1 ½ pounds venison loin steak, about 1-inch thick, trimmed of all fat and connective tissue

3 tablespoons Crazy Cajun seasoning (see page 158)

4 ounces Boursin cheese (herbed cream cheese)

4 flour tortillas, 12 inches in diameter

Grilled Moose Flank Steak With Shallots

. . . .

SERVES: 6

PREP TIME: 10 MINUTES

COOKING TIME: 20 MINUTES

2 tablespoons olive oil

13 shallots, peeled and cut into thin slices

1½ teaspoons Italian seasoning (or a mixture of oregano, thyme, and rosemary)

¼ teaspoon freshly ground black pepper

½ cup dry white wine

kosher salt and freshly ground pepper, to taste

1½ pounds of flank steak, trimmed of all fat and connective tissue

Moose meat is savored in our household, so there isn't much of the meat that goes to waste or into a burger if we can prevent it! It has a slightly sweeter taste than other venison. Here's a flavorful method for preparing moose or any other type of venison flank.

Add 1 tablespoon of oil to a sauté pan over medium heat. Place the shallots in and cook until they are softened, about 3 minutes. Add the herbs, pepper, and white wine. Cover and let simmer for about 5 minutes. Uncover and let simmer until the liquid is reduced by half. When reduced, season with salt and pepper and set aside.

Preheat the grill for about 20 minutes. The grill should be hot enough that you can hold your hand over it for only a few seconds.

Bring the flank steak to room temperature. Blot it dry with paper towels and brush it lightly with the remaining olive oil.

Place the flank steak on the grill and let it cook for about 3 minutes. Turn and cook an additional 3 to 5 minutes, depending upon the thickness of the flank. Brush with oil while the second side cooks. Grill until medium-rare.

Remove the steak from the grill to let it set for a minute or two. While the moose flank is resting, reheat the sauce. Slice the flank against the grain and pour the sauce over the slices. Serve immediately.

Hint: The quickest way to peel shallots or garlic is to first separate the head into cloves. I place the cloves on a flat surface (such as the cutting board), place the side of a butcher's knife on top of the clove, hold the handle with my right hand, and then press down hard with my left hand on the flat side of the blade against the clove. As the cloves crush, the skin separates easily.

Is It Hot Enough?

If you don't have a thermometer on your grill, here's a pretty reliable way to gauge the heat. (And you'll impress your friends when you simply hold your hand over the grill and declare the proper temperature without any other aid!) Hold your hand just above the grill where you plan to cook the food. The length of time that you can hold it there comfortably will be your gauge of the grill temperature.

SECONDS OVER GRILL	COAL/GRILL TEMPERATURE
1 to 2	Hot
3	Medium-hot
4	Medium
5	Medium-low
6	Low

One-for-the-Road Moose Ribs

Moose ribs have much more meat than do deer ribs. This recipe is a weekend favorite when I can keep an eye on them cooking and enjoy the pungent wafts of smoke from the grill.

SERVES: 6 TO 8

PREP TIME: 10 MINUTES

MARINATING TIME: 6 TO 12 HOURS

COOKING TIME: 2_ HOURS

In a blender or food processor, combine 18 ounces of the beer (keep the remaining 6 ounces cold), onion, tomatoes, Worcestershire sauce, thyme, garlic, and hot sauce. Blend until no chunks are present.

Place the ribs in a nonmetallic container and pour the sauce over them. Turn the ribs to coat thoroughly. It may save some space in the refrigerator if you place the ribs in large, zip-lock plastic bags and cover them with the marinade. Let them sit for 6 to 12 hours.

Preheat the grill with the lid closed until it reaches about 250°F. Place the ribs and the marinade in a large, disposable aluminum pan. I like to use two pans set inside one another when there is a lot of weight involved. Cover the pan with foil and place it on the grill. Close the lid. Let it cook on the grill for about 2½ hours, until the meat falls off the rib bones easily. Check occasionally and turn any ribs that are not covered with the barbecue liquid.

While the ribs cook, sit back and enjoy the remaining glass (6 ounces) of beer.

24 ounces Honey Brown lager (or any ale will do)

1 large onion, cut into chunks

1 can diced tomatoes, drained

3 tablespoons Worcestershire sauce

½ teaspoon dried thyme

5 garlic cloves, minced

1 teaspoon hot sauce, such as Tabasco

4 to 6 pounds moose ribs, trimmed of all fat and connective tissue

Scrumptious Doe Burgers

SERVES: 4

PREP TIME: 5 MINUTES

COOKING TIME: 15 TO 20 MINUTES

2 pounds ground venison

4 slices bacon, cooked and
  crumbled

2 tablespoons scallions, minced

½ teaspoon garlic salt

¼ teaspoon pepper

4 ounces herbed cheese,
  such as Boursin

heavy cream, as needed

2 teaspoons canola oil

Since venison is inherently a low-fat meat, it is important to ensure that when it is cooked, the process is as even as possible. When cooking burgers, make sure that the meat is at room temperature prior to placing it on the grill.

Preheat the grill for about 20 minutes. The grill should be hot enough that you can hold your hand over it for only a few seconds.

In a medium bowl, combine the venison, bacon, scallions, garlic salt, and pepper. Mix thoroughly and shape into 4 patties.

In another small bowl, beat the cheese until smooth, adding a little cream if necessary. Split each burger patty almost in half, as if you were butterflying them. Dollop ¼ of the cheese mixture into the middle of the patty (keeping it away from the edge of the burger) and fold over the top of the burger. Seal the edges with wet fingers.

Lightly brush each patty with canola oil to prevent them from sticking to the grill. Place all four burgers in a hinged grill basket and cook to desired doneness, about 6 to 8 minutes each side.

Burgers Italiano Sans Bun

Here's a zesty alternative to regular hamburgers that has an Italian flair. If you love cheese, feel free to add some grated mozzarella on top of the burgers during their last few minutes of grilling. If necessary, the sauce for the burgers can be made one day before you prepare the burgers.

Preheat the grill for about 20 minutes. The grill should be hot enough that you can hold your hand over it for only a few seconds.

Prepare the tomato sauce ahead of time. In a small saucepan, heat the oil over medium heat. Add the garlic and sauté until golden brown. Do not burn. Add the tomatoes and oregano and simmer for about 5 minutes. Season to taste with salt and pepper. Keep warm.

In a bowl, combine the venison, cheese, bread crumbs, egg, onion, olives, parsley, and oregano. Form into six patties. Lightly brush the patties with oil to prevent them from sticking to the grill.

Place the patties in a hinged grill basket and grill until done, about 5 minutes each side, depending upon the thickness of the burger.

Place each burger on a plate and top with the warmed tomato sauce. Serve immediately.

SERVES 6

PREP TIME: 20 MINUTES

COOKING TIME: 10 MINUTES

Sauce:

2 tablespoons olive oil

1 tablespoon garlic, minced

1 ½ cups canned plum tomatoes (with juice placed in food processor to chop)

oregano, salt, and pepper, to taste

1 ½ pounds ground venison

½ cup Parmesan cheese, grated

2 cups fresh bread crumbs

1 egg

¼ cup onion, minced

2 tablespoons black olives, minced

¼ cup fresh parsley, chopped

1 tablespoon dried oregano

¼ cup olive oil

Herb Garden Venison Burger

SERVES: 4

PREP TIME: 5 MINUTES

COOKING TIME: 10 MINUTES

The grilled burger is as much a barbecue mainstay today as it was decades ago. There's something about grilling burgers that brings a sense of blissfulness to all who partake in the grilling and/or the eating! Here is a simple venison burger recipe that works well with pure ground venison. If you prefer to stay with ground venison with 10 to 15 percent pork fat, you can omit the soft butter during grilling and place the burgers directly on the grill without a hinged grilling rack.

1 to 1½ pounds ground venison

¼ cup red onion, finely chopped

2 teaspoons Italian seasoning (or dried herbs such as basil and oregano)

freshly ground black pepper, to taste

salt, to taste

unsalted butter, softened

4 kaiser rolls or hamburger buns, split

4 slices red onion

Preheat the grill for about 20 minutes. The grill should be hot enough that you can hold your hand over it for only a few seconds.

In a large bowl, hand mix the ground venison, chopped onion, seasoning, and black pepper to taste. Shape into four patties, no more than 1 inch thick. Make sure that the patties are at room temperature before grilling.

Place the patties onto an oiled, hinged grill basket. Place over the grill and cook for 3 to 4 minutes. While the burgers are cooking, place a small amount of butter on top of the burgers. Turn the grill basket over and while the other side is cooking, place a small amount of butter on the burgers and season with salt on the sides that have already cooked. Grill the burgers an additional 3 to 4 minutes. Remove from the grill.

During the last few minutes, as the burgers cook, spread a little butter on the inside of the cut kaiser rolls and grill on a cooler part of the grill for 1 minute.

Place the sliced onions on the buns, and top with the burgers. Add condiments such as mayonnaise, ketchup, relish, mustard, or horseradish sauce, as you desire.

Venison Blue Cheese Burgers

This recipe will lift a classic venison burger up a step. The full-bodied flavor of the blue cheese butter nicely compliments the grilled venison.

Preheat the grill for about 20 minutes. The grill should be hot enough that you can hold your hand over it for only a few seconds.

Combine the ground venison, Worcestershire sauce, salt, and pepper. Mix thoroughly, but quickly. Too much handling of the meat will make it fall apart. Shape the venison into 4 burgers.

Place each burger into an oiled, hinged grill basket and place on the grill. Let them cook about 3 minutes on each side. While they are cooking, lightly toast the rolls on the upper shelf or cooler part of the grill. When the burgers are done, place each one on the bottom half of a bun. Place a slice of blue cheese butter on top of each of the burgers, followed by a slice of tomato. Add the bun top and serve immediately.

SERVES: 4

PREP TIME: 5 MINUTES

COOKING TIME: 6 MINUTES

1 pound ground venison

1 tablespoon Worcestershire sauce

salt and freshly ground pepper, to taste

4 slices Blue Cheese Butter (see page 154)

4 kaiser rolls or hamburger buns, split

4 slices beef tomatoes

Roasted Garlic "Buck" Rub Burgers

SERVES: 6

PREP TIME: 10 MINUTES

COOKING TIME: 50 MINUTES

1½ heads of garlic, with a little of the tops cut off

olive oil, as needed

2 pounds ground venison

1 egg

1 tablespoon Worcestershire sauce

1 teaspoon kosher salt

1 teaspoon freshly ground black pepper

6 kaiser rolls or hamburger buns, split

Garlic is one of the most helpful members of the onion family. It's health benefits range from lowering cholesterol to keeping your heart healthy to warding off illnesses. You'll love the aroma from these garlicky burgers as they cook on the grill.

Preheat the oven to 350°F. Rub the top of the garlic heads with oil. Place in a small casserole dish or wrap loosely with foil, leaving the top open. Bake for about 40 minutes. Remove from oven and let cool. (Note: this can be done the day before).

Preheat the grill for about 20 minutes. The grill should be hot enough that you can hold your hand over it for only a few seconds.

When the garlic heads are cool, squeeze the garlic from the skins and place the cloves in a bowl and mix them with the remaining ingredients. Form patties loosely. Coat lightly with oil before placing them on the grill.

Grill the burgers for about 4 to 5 minutes per side. Toast the buns lightly on a cooler section of the grill. Serve with mayonnaise, ketchup, relish, mustard, and other standard burger accompaniments.

Mis en Place for Grilling

Mis en place is the French term for "everything in its place." While this is an essential element for all types of cooking, it is especially critical when grilling. Since the cooking happens quickly, go through all recipes and figure out which ones will take the longest. Prepare all your other dishes before the first one goes on the grill. Have all your cooking utensils ready and serving dishes out, too.

Smoky Cheese Venison Burgers

I often proclaim these burgers as gourmet venison cheese-burgers—they are absolutely mouth-watering.

SERVES: 6

PREP TIME: 10 MINUTES

COOKING TIME: 10 MINUTES

Preheat the grill for about 20 minutes. The grill should be hot enough that you can hold your hand over it for only a few seconds.

Form the venison patties loosely with the ground venison. Coat both the venison patties and the onion slices lightly with oil before placing them on the grill.

Grill the burgers for about 4 to 5 minutes per side. The onions will probably be done a little more quickly. Season both the burgers and the onion slices with salt and pepper before turning them.

Brush the cut sides of the rolls or buns with butter and place cut side down on a cooler section of the grill. Just before the burgers are done, place a slice of smoked cheese on top and place the top half of the roll. Let grill for about 30 seconds and remove to the bottom part of the roll.

Serve with mayonnaise, ketchup, relish, mustard, or other standard burger accompaniments.

2 pounds ground venison

6 slices Walla Walla, Vidalia, or other sweet onion

¼ cup unsalted butter or canola oil

salt and pepper, to taste

6 kaiser rolls or hamburger buns, split

6 slices smoked Gouda or mozzarella cheese

Tortilla Mushroom Burgers

SERVES: 6

PREP TIME: 20 MINUTES

COOKING TIME: 15 MINUTES

2 teaspoons unsalted butter

1 cup fresh mushrooms, sliced

salt and pepper, to taste

1½ pounds ground venison

2 tablespoons canola oil

12 flour tortillas, 6 inches in diameter

1 large red or green bell pepper, roasted, peeled, and cut into long thin strips

½ pound Monterey Jack cheese, shredded

1 cup Sizzlin' Fresh Tomato Salsa (see page 138) or any other tomato-based salsa, such as Imus or Picante

For those who love tortillas or dislike thick hamburger buns, this recipe is a meal in itself. To make the final assembly go smoothly, be sure all your ingredients are near the grill.

Preheat the grill for about 20 minutes. The grill should be hot enough that you can hold your hand over it for only a few seconds.

In a skillet over medium heat, melt the butter. Add the mushrooms and let cook about 5 minutes. Remove from heat, season with salt and pepper, and set aside. This can be done the day before, but make sure to refrigerate the mushrooms overnight and then bring to room temperature before cooking the burgers.

Carefully form the ground venison into 6 thin patties, no more than ½ inch thick. Season with salt and pepper. Lightly brush the burgers with oil before placing them on the grill. Cook for about 3 to 4 minutes each side. Set burgers aside on a platter.

Place a tortilla on a cooler section of the grill and top with some of the mushrooms and roasted peppers. Place one burger on top and then top with some of the shredded cheese. Place another tortilla on top of the cheese and press lightly. Let this cook on the grill a few minutes, and then carefully turn and let it cook on the grill only about 1 minute more. Set aside and keep warm. Repeat this for the remaining tortilla burgers. Cut each burger in half and serve with salsa, sour cream, chips, and some ice cold beer.

Summer Avocado Venison Burgers

When buying an avocado, select one with unbroken skin and a heavy feel for its size. The California variety with thick black skin is best during the summer and fall. Allow it to ripen at home on a window sill. You should be able to smell its fragrance when it's ripe. Mixed with yoghurt, the avocado's delicate flavor is a tasty light topping for these summer burgers.

SERVES: 4
PREP TIME: 15 MINUTES
COOKING TIME: 8 MINUTES

Preheat the grill for about 20 minutes. The grill should be hot enough that you can hold your hand over it for only a few seconds.

Combine the venison, onion, parsley, Worcestershire sauce, salt, and pepper. Form into 4 patties.

In a small bowl, mash the avocado with the yoghurt, lemon, and lime juice. Season with salt and pepper. Set aside.

Lightly oil the hinged grill basket and place the four burgers inside. Grill the burgers for about 3 to 4 minutes each side. Just before the burgers are done, lightly toast the rolls or buns on a cooler section of the grill.

Place each burger on the bottom half of each bun and top with the avocado mixture. To spice it up a bit, top with a splash of Tabasco or other hot sauce! Serve immediately.

1 pound ground venison

3 tablespoons onion, grated

2 tablespoons parsley, chopped

Worcestershire sauce, to taste

salt and freshly ground pepper, to taste

1 ripe avocado, peeled and pitted

2 tablespoons plain non-fat yoghurt

1 teaspoon lemon juice

½ teaspoon lime juice

4 kaiser rolls or hamburger buns, split

hinged grill basket

2 tablespoons canola oil

Thai Pita Burgers

SERVES: 4 OR 5

PREP TIME: 15 MINUTES

COOKING TIME: 10 MINUTES

1 pound ground venison

3 tablespoons Asian peanut sauce

2 scallions (green onions), finely chopped

1 teaspoon fresh gingerroot, grated

salt and pepper, to taste

1 tablespoon canola oil

4 or 5 large pita halves

There are many interesting elements of Asian cooking. The aromatic blend of peanut sauce, onions, and gingerroot makes for a very appealing twist on venison burgers.

Preheat the grill for about 20 minutes. The grill should be hot enough that you can hold your hand over it for only a few seconds.

In a bowl, gently combine the venison, peanut sauce, scallions, and gingerroot. Season with salt and pepper.

Shape into 4 or 5 patties. Lightly brush the patties with oil. Place in a hinged grill basket and grill about 3 to 4 minutes per side.

Toast the pita halves on a cooler section of the grill and then place the burgers inside. Top each burger with a slice of fresh tomato.

Prepare Your Cooking Surfaces

Whether your are cooking on a grate or on a griddle, make sure they are clean and lightly oiled. Before cooking, let the cooking surface heat up with the lid closed for about 20 minutes, and then scrape away any leftover food particles with a brush. Next, lightly oil the grate or griddle to prevent food from sticking. When you're done grilling, turn the heat up to high, and scrub away any leftover food particles with a wire brush. These few steps will keep your grill in better shape and will make it easier to cook with the next time around.

Barbecued Bacon Burgers

I call this my "All-American" burger. I've served it to folks who never knew they were eating venison.

SERVES: 6

PREP TIME: 5 MINUTES

COOKING TIME: 10 MINUTES

In a large bowl, gently mix the ground venison, barbecue sauce, bread crumbs, and pepper. Form 6 patties and wrap 1 piece of bacon around each patty. Secure the bacon with a toothpick.

Brush the hinged grill basket with oil and place the burgers inside. (A hinged grill basket comes in handy for this recipe to make sure that the bacon does not fall off into the grill). Grill for about 2 to 3 minutes each side. Be careful of any flare-ups from the bacon grease dripping off the burgers. When done, set the burgers aside while toasting the cut side of the rolls on a cooler part of the grill.

Top each burger with sliced onion, tomato, or sautéed mushrooms.

1 ½ pounds ground venison

2 tablespoons prepared barbecue sauce (I like Uncle Buck's Original Barbecue Sauce, but your own favorite will do)

¼ cup plain bread crumbs

freshly ground pepper, to taste

6 strips bacon

toothpicks

1 tablespoon canola oil

hinged grill basket

6 kaiser rolls or hamburger buns, split

Savory Venison Phyllo Triangles

YIELD: 25 TRIANGLES

PREP TIME: 10 MINUTES

ASSEMBLY TIME: 45 MINUTES

COOKING TIME: 40 MINUTES

1 pound spicy fresh venison sausage

1 clove shallots

1 cup onion, finely chopped

1 cup heavy cream, room temperature

1 tablespoon Dijon-style mustard

⅛ teaspoon grated nutmeg

¼ cup chives, finely chopped

10 sheets of phyllo, 17 by 12 inches each

½ cup unsalted butter, melted

This is one of my favorite appetizers.

In a large skillet over medium heat, sauté the sausage with the shallots and onion until cooked thoroughly. Drain the mixture in a colander and transfer it to paper towels to drain additionally. Once drained, combine the sausage mixture, cream, mustard, and nutmeg and simmer the mixture, stirring occasionally, for 10 to 12 minutes or until it is very thick and mounds on a spoon. Stir in the chives and let the mixture cool.

Place a sheet of the phyllo on a work surface with a long side facing you and brush it lightly with butter. Place a second sheet of phyllo over the first one and brush it lightly with some of the remaining butter. (Note: Keep a damp towel on top of the phyllo that is set aside to prevent it from drying out.)

Cut the sheets crosswise into 5 equal strips, each about 3½ inches wide. Place 1 tablespoon of the filling about 1 inch from the bottom of the strip; fold the lower right-hand corner of the strip up over the filling, forming a triangle. Brush the top of the triangle with some butter. Continue to fold the filled triangle up the entire length of the strip, brushing it lightly with more butter after each fold.

Repeat this process with the remaining strips and place the phyllo triangles on a baking sheet. Make phyllo triangles in the same manner with the remaining 8 phyllo sheets and place them on baking sheets as they are formed. Bake the filled triangles in the middle of a preheated 350°F oven for 25 to 30 minutes or until puffed and golden. Makes about 25 phyllo triangles.

Don't Forget Me

Remember to frequently check food for doneness. Since grilling is a quick high-heat method of dry cooking, food cooks rather quickly. Keep in mind that there will be some carry-over cooking after the food is removed from the heat of the grill. You don't want to overcook any food because there is no turning back! Undercooked food can always be put back onto the fire.

One-Pan Venison Sausage Dinner

This one-dish meal is great for weeknight cooking or if you have been out all day on the weekend and want to fix something that's filling and yet easy to prepare. Prep all the ingredients in the morning and this will be even quicker to cook at dinnertime.

SERVES: 4

PREP: 10 MINUTES

COOK TIME: 30 MINUTES

Heat oil in a large skillet over medium-high heat. Add the potatoes and season with salt and pepper. Cover and cook 8 to 10 minutes, stirring occasionally, until potatoes are browned. Stir in the onions and peppers and cook until the onions are translucent. Remove from pan.

With heat still on medium-high, add the broccoli and chicken broth. Stir and cook the broccoli for about 5 minutes. Add back in the potatoes, onions, and peppers. Stir in the venison sausage. Cover and cook about 15 minutes or until the venison is cooked through, stirring occasionally. Sprinkle with cheese and cover until the cheese is melted.

3 tablespoons canola oil

¾ pound diced red or white potatoes

¼ pound white onions, diced

1 green bell pepper, seeded, diced

¼ teaspoon salt

½ teaspoon pepper

2 cups broccoli florets

¼ cup chicken broth

1 pound venison smoked sausage

1 cup cheddar cheese, shredded

Venison Sausage 'n' Peppers Grinder

SERVES: 4

PREP TIME: 15 MINUTES

COOKING TIME: 25 MINUTES

Combining venison sausage and grilling is a win-win situation. The flavor of the charcoal-grilled casing of the sausage along with the delicious taste of the spiced venison mixture is perfect on a cool summer or fall evening. I usually take out the sausage in the morning, let it defrost, and prepare the vegetables and sauce. This way, in the evening, there's not much more to be bothered with other than keeping an eye on the sausage while it grills (and perhaps sipping a cocktail).

4 large links of venison sausage, prepared hot Italian style

2 tablespoons canola oil

2 green peppers, seeded and sliced into strips

2 white onions, sliced into thin strips

½ cup tomato sauce

salt and pepper, to taste

1 to 2 loaves of French bread, cut into lengths equal to the sausage

2 cups mozzarella cheese, grated

Preheat the grill for about 20 minutes. The grill should be hot enough that you can hold your hand over it for only a few seconds.

Place the sausages on the grill and turn occasionally to prevent burning. Grill until seared on all sides, about 7 to 10 minutes, depending upon the intensity of the heat. If using a gas grill, lower the heat to medium. If using coals, place the sausage on a slightly cooler section of the grill. Next, cook the sausages over a lower heat for another 10 minutes, in order to cook them thoroughly.

While the sausages are grilling, heat the oil in a medium skillet over medium-high heat. Sauté the onions and peppers until they are soft and cooked through, about 5 to 7 minutes. Add the tomato sauce and let simmer about 3 minutes.

Season to taste with salt and pepper. Remove from heat and keep warm.

Split the French bread lengthwise, place 1 link of sausage split lengthwise on half of the bread, and top with the peppers, onion, and tomato sauce mixture.

Sprinkle the top with grated mozzarella cheese, place on the warming grill, and close the lid to let the cheese melt.

Remove from grill, fold over the sandwich top and serve.

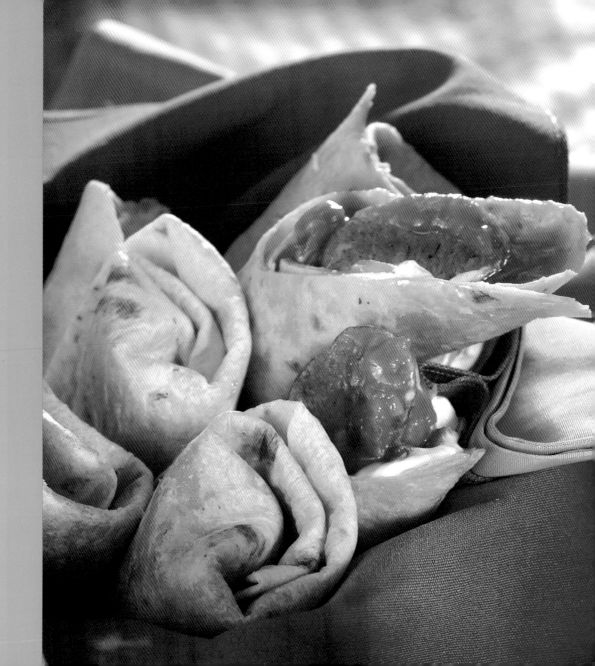

Grilled Venison Sausage Wrap

Venison is a lean meat, and sometimes the sausage made from it can be on the dry side. The salsa in this recipe adds both moisture and a complementary flavor to the cooked sausage.

Preheat the grill for about 20 minutes. The grill should be hot enough that you can hold your hand over it for only a few seconds.

Lightly oil the sausages before placing them on the grill. Grill the sausages uncovered for about 5 to 7 minutes until they have a crisp outer skin. Move to a slightly cooler section of the grill and cook an additional 15 minutes or so, until cooked all the way through.

When done, set aside the sausages on a platter to let the juices set. In the meantime, take each tortilla and heat them on the grill. With a pair of tongs, place one tortilla at a time on the grill and turn after 10 seconds, depending how hot the grill is. Let it cook on the other side no more than 5 seconds and place it back on a platter. Repeat the process for the remaining tortillas.

Place each grilled sausage on the heated tortillas and top with some salsa. Fold in the sides and roll up. Serve immediately.

SERVES: 6

PREP TIME: 5 MINUTES

COOKING TIME: 20 TO 25 MINUTES

6 uncooked venison sausage links, 6 ounces each, room temperature

2 tablespoons canola oil

6 flour tortillas, 12 inches in diameter, plain or seasoned, such as tomato-basil or garlic-herb.

2 cups Sizzlin' Tomato Salsa (see page 138) or any other tomato-based salsa, such as Imus or Picante

Dijon Venison Sausage Kebobs

SERVES: 4 TO 5

PREP TIME: 15 MINUTES

MARINATING TIME: 1 HOUR

COOKING TIME: 10 MINUTES

2 tablespoons canola oil

3 tablespoons Dijon-style mustard

½ teaspoon dried crushed thyme

1 teaspoon white wine vinegar

2 pounds venison sausage, cut in 1-inch chunks

8 to 10 button mushroom caps

1 large red pepper, seeded and cut into 1-inch squares

1 large onion, cut into 1-inch chunks

4 or 5 metal skewers or bamboo skewers soaked in cold water for 1 hour.

The smooth, hot, sharp taste of Dijon mustard makes an aromatic and flavorful marinade for this recipe.

In a shallow, non-reactive dish, mix the canola oil, mustard, thyme, and vinegar. Add the sausage, mushrooms, pepper, and onion. Stir to coat all pieces thoroughly. (This can also be done in a large zip-lock plastic bag.) Marinate for about 1 hour.

Preheat the grill for about 20 minutes. The grill should be hot enough that you can hold your hand over it for only a few seconds.

Thread the sausage, mushrooms, pepper, and onion alternately on the skewers. Place the kebobs on the grill and cook for 7 to 10 minutes until cooked throughout. Turn occasionally and baste with any remaining mustard marinade while cooking. Serve immediately.

Think Safety

Keep a fire extinguisher or a large
box of baking soda near the grill. In
case there is a flare-up, you'll want to
be able to put it out before anything
drastic occurs. Also, keep small chil-
dren and pets away from the grill.

Grilled Venison Hot Dogs Supreme

Who knew that one day there would be a fad for gourmet hot dogs? Toppings today are no longer just plain catsup, mustard, relish, and/or sauerkraut; they now include chili, mashed garlic potatoes, sour cream and chives, stewed onions, roasted peppers, and more. This homemade relish will bring your venison hot dogs to the next level!

SERVES: 3
PREP TIME: 10 MINUTES
COOKING TIME: 10 MINUTES

Preheat the grill for about 20 minutes. The grill should be hot enough that you can hold your hand over it for only a few seconds.

In a small bowl, combine the tomato, scallion, garlic, corn, red onion, olive oil, and vinegar. Season with salt and pepper. Add oil and vinegar to your preference, if necessary.

Place the hot dogs on a section of the grill just slightly away from the hottest part. Since venison hot dogs are usually not as moist as regular ones, they can not take the extreme high heat that regular hot dogs can. I like to use a hinged grilling basket with venison hot dogs to turn them frequently on the grill (without losing them through the slots!).

Place the hot dog buns, split side down, on a cooler section of the grill to slightly toast them. When done, place the grilled hot dogs in the buns and top with the supreme relish!

1 fresh tomato, seeded and finely chopped

1 stalk scallion (green onion), finely chopped

1 clove garlic, minced

¼ cup corn kernels, diced

¼ cup red onion, diced

¼ cup olive oil

2 tablespoons red wine vinegar

salt and pepper, to taste

6 venison hot dogs

6 hot dog buns, split

Grilled Sausage Wrap

SERVES: 4

PREP TIME: 20 MINUTES

COOKING TIME: 20 TO 30 MINUTES

1 ¼ cup Italian dressing

1 eggplant, cut in lengthwise slices

1 zucchini, cut in lengthwise slices

2 red bell peppers, cut into wedges

1 red onion, cut into ½-inch slices

2 metal skewers or bamboo skewers soaked in cold water for 1 hour

4 venison sausages

4 large tortillas, 12 inches in diameter

1 tomato, sliced

The marinated vegetables add another scrumptious dimension to this grilled sausage recipe.

Preheat the grill for about 20 minutes. The grill should be hot enough that you can hold your hand over it for only a few seconds.

In a large bowl, combine one cup of the dressing, eggplant, zucchini, and red bell peppers. Mix to coat thoroughly. Thread the onion slices on the metal skewers. (This prevents the onion slices from coming apart when turning them.)

Place the sausages on the grill and cook to crisp the outside skin, about 3 to 5 minutes. Turn occasionally. Move to a cooler section of the grill to continue cooking.

While the sausages are cooking on a cooler section of the grill, begin cooking the vegetables. In batches, remove the vegetables from the dressing and grill them until lightly browned on both sides. Brush the onion slices with some of the dressing before placing on the grill. Grill until slightly brown on each side. Set aside and keep warm.

When the venison sausages are almost done, heat up the tortillas on the grill. Place the tortilla on the grill and heat for about 15 to 30 seconds each side.

Slice the sausages lengthwise, place two halves in the middle of each tortilla, layer with some grilled vegetables and tomato slices. Drizzle with a little of the remaining Italian dressing (not the amount used for marinating) on the sausage and vegetables and roll up the tortilla. Serve warm.

Venison Sausage Omelet Delight

YIELDS: 2 OMELETS

PREP TIME: 15 MINUTES

COOKING TIME: 15 MINUTES

⅓ pound bulk venison sausage

4 tablespoons butter
(2 and 1 and 1)

⅓ cup fresh mushrooms,
chopped

2 tablespoons onion, finely
minced

4 eggs (2 and 2)

2 tablespoons milk (1 and 1)

salt and pepper, to taste

¼ cup mozzarella cheese,
shredded

I often prepare this filling breakfast recipe during the cold, snowy winter months. It really hits the spot after a morning of shoveling and plowing the snow.

In a small skillet, sauté the sausage until it is browned. Remove the sausage and set aside.

Melt the 2 tablespoons butter in the skillet and sauté the mushrooms and onions over medium heat. Sauté until much of the juice from the mushrooms has been cooked out, about 5 to 7 minutes. Set the mushroom/onion mixture aside and keep warm.

In a small bowl, combine 2 eggs, 1 tablespoon of milk, and salt and pepper to taste. Beat gently with a fork until just blended. Melt 1 teaspoon of the butter in an omelet pan over medium heat (when the heat is too high, the egg toughens too quickly). When the butter begins to sizzle, add the egg mixture and tilt the pan to spread the eggs over the bottom. As soon as the eggs set on the bottom, pull the cooked egg from the edge of the pan with a rubber spatula and tilt the pan to let the liquid egg flow underneath to cook. Set the pan back on the range top to continue cooking, repeat the process if necessary.

Sprinkle half of the cooked venison sausage, half of the mushroom/onion mixture, and half of the cheese over one half of the omelet. Tilt the pan to one side and fold over the "empty" half of the omelet with a rubber spatula. Cover the omelet pan with a lid (or piece of foil) for 20 to 30 seconds to make sure all the cheese has melted. Remove, plate, and serve with hot biscuits and butter.

Cook the second omelet following the same procedures as the first.

CHAPTER TWO

Chili'n'

CHILIES
CHILI AS A MAIN INGREDIENT

This section contains both chili recipes and recipes that include chili as a main ingredient. Over the years, I have intentionally prepared large batches of chili to have some of it remain as a leftover. Yet there is no doubt that a certain amount of magic occurs when chili rests overnight in the refrigerator and is heated up again the next day—there's not much better tasting chili than day-old chili. Its flavors blend together to create a unique and satisfying mélange that somehow cannot be achieved on the first day of its creation.

The chilies I have included vary from those with beans to those without beans, to fast-fix chili to slow-cooked classics, and some spicy chilies, too. The recipes that follow those include different ways to use day-old chili. Use it in a casserole, burrito, quesadilla, strudel, or tostada—you can even make it into mini cupcakes! Cupcakes? Turn the pages—you'll see.

No Bean Chunky Chili

SERVES: 6

PREP TIME: 20 MINUTES

COOKING TIME: 1½ HOURS

Many chili purists claim that a "real" chili doesn't have beans. Yet, other die-hard chili lovers claim it isn't chili without them. While several of my recipes do include them (you guessed which side I'm on)—here's a flavorful and spicy chunky chili without the beans. Enjoy!

4 tablespoons canola oil (2 and 2)

2 pounds venison stew meat, cut into ½-inch cubes

¼ cup red wine

1 can (6 ounces) tomato paste

2 onions, chopped

6 cloves garlic, minced

1 tablespoon dried oregano

2 teaspoons ground cumin

4 tablespoons ground chile powder

1 teaspoon salt (I like ground kosher salt)

1 teaspoon freshly ground black pepper

½ teaspoon cayenne pepper

2 cups diced, canned plum tomatoes with the juice

1½ cups beer, room temperature (to keep the Mexican flare, try Corona)

In a Dutch oven, heat 2 tablespoons of the oil over high heat. Add some of the venison and cook quickly to brown it on all sides. Cook the remaining venison in batches. Set aside. Drain any liquid from the Dutch oven.

Place the red wine in a medium glass bowl and stir in the can of tomato paste. Mix well until the wine is thoroughly combined with the tomato paste. Set aside.

Heat the remaining oil in the Dutch oven over medium-high heat. Add the onions and cook until soft, about 10 minutes. Add the garlic, oregano, cumin, chile powder, salt, black pepper, and cayenne pepper. Stir and cook for about two minutes. Stir in the tomato paste mixture, tomatoes and the liquid, and the beer. Add in the cooked venison and mix well. Bring the mixture to a boil; reduce heat and let simmer covered, about 1 hour.

Serve warm with side accompaniments such as minced onion, sour cream, grated cheddar cheese, or large tortilla dipping chips!

Quick-Fix Venison Chili

When time is short, this is a great meal to prepare. While it simmers, heat up some refrigerated biscuits (such as Pillsbury) in the oven, read the day's mail, set the table, and sip a nice cocktail!

SERVES: 8

PREP TIME: 20 MINUTES

COOKING TIME: 45 MINUTES

In a large stock pot or Dutch oven, sauté the onion in the canola oil over medium heat. When the onions are translucent, add in the garlic. Continue sautéing until the garlic begins to turn slightly golden. Add in the ground venison and continue to cook. Stir to break up the venison and cook until all the meat is browned. Add in the remaining ingredients. As you add in the tomatoes, break up the whole ones with your fingers (or with a knife, if you prefer). Stir the mixture to blend the ingredients well. Heat to a gentle simmer, stirring occasionally. Cover and simmer 45 minutes. Serve with grated cheddar cheese.

1 large onion, chopped

1 tablespoon canola oil

4 cloves garlic, minced

2 ½ pounds lean ground venison

1 can (15 ounces) kidney beans, drained

1 can (11 ounces) corn, drained

1 can (28 ounces) whole tomatoes with juice

2 tablespoons chile powder

2 teaspoons cumin

1 teaspoon salt

¼ teaspoon cayenne pepper

Uncle Buck's "Three" Step Black Bean Chili

SERVES: 3

PREP TIME: 5 MINUTES

COOKING TIME: 30 MINUTES

This ready-made product is a must-have for all kitchen cooks who, from time to time, receive unexpected guests for meals at the last minute. While Uncle Buck's products (from Bass Pro Shops) are top quality across the board, this is one of my favorites. Ground venison, a can of tomato sauce, and water are all that you need to prepare this delicious chili. I like to add some corn to make it even thicker!

1½ pounds ground venison (I like meaty chili)

3⅓ cups water

1 can (15 ounces) tomato sauce

1 bottle/bag (6 ounces) Uncle Buck's Two Step Black Bean Chili

1 cup corn (either canned or frozen)

In a skillet over medium heat, brown the venison. Drain and set aside.

In a Dutch oven, add in the water, tomato sauce, and chili mix. Stir well to combine thoroughly. Add the browned venison. Bring to a simmer over medium-high heat. Lower heat—but keep it at a simmer for 30 minutes. For the last 15 minutes, add in the corn. Stir occasionally.

Sloppy Does

Much like chili that can cook on low heat all day in the crock pot, so does this recipe for Sloppy Does. It can also be prepared, however, in less than an hour on the stove top if time is short.

YIELDS: 8 SANDWICHES

PREP TIME: 15 MINUTES

COOKING TIME: 8 HOURS,

SLOW COOKING

In a large skillet over medium heat, cook the venison, onion, and garlic until the meat is browned. While the venison is cooking, combine the remaining ingredients (except for the buns) in a slow-cooker or crock pot. Stir to mix well. Add in the meat mixture when it is done and mix thoroughly. Cover and cook on low for 6 to 8 hours. If the mixture is too watery, take the lid off for the last hour or so to thicken it up.

Lightly toast or grill the buns and spoon the mixture over them.

1 ½ pounds ground venison

1 cup onion, chopped

3 cloves garlic, minced

1 cup chile sauce

½ cup green pepper, chopped

¼ cup celery, chopped

½ cup mushrooms, chopped

¼ cup water

2 tablespoons light brown sugar

2 tablespoons prepared mustard

2 tablespoons red wine vinegar

2 tablespoons Worcestershire sauce

2 teaspoons chile powder

8 hamburger buns, split

Santa Fe Venison Chili

SERVES: 4 TO 6

PREP TIME: 25 MINUTES

COOKING TIME: 1½ HOURS

½ cup canola oil

2 pounds venison, chopped, trimmed of all fat and connective tissue

8 cloves garlic, minced

1 onion, chopped

2 tablespoons chipotle peppers in adobo sauce

5 medium tomatoes, seeded and chopped

1 teaspoon ground cumin

1 tablespoon Mexican oregano

2 cups water

2 cups beef stock

salt and freshly ground pepper, to taste

Chipotle peppers are ripe jalapeno chiles that have been dried and then smoked. They are found canned in red tomato sauce in most ethnic sections of grocery stores.

Heat the oil in a Dutch oven over medium-high heat. Add in the venison, garlic, and onion. Stir frequently to prevent the meat from lumping together (cook in batches if your pan is not large enough). Cook until meat has browned, about 10 minutes. Add the chipotle puree, tomatoes, cumin, oregano, water, and beef stock. Bring to a simmer, uncovered, and let cook for 1 to 1½ hours, stirring occasionally. Season with salt and pepper to taste. Serve hot with accompaniments of sour cream, grated cheddar cheese, corn bread, and butter.

Venison Chile Pepper Con Carne

If you love cooking with a variety of chile peppers, then this recipe will suit your fancy. The prep is a tad bit longer, but well worth the effort. It's venison chili with plenty of chile peppers!

SERVES: 6 TO 8

PREP TIME: 20 MINUTES

COOKING TIME: 45 MINUTES

Rinse the dried chiles and place in a small saucepan with the water. Bring to a boil. Reduce the heat to medium-low and let simmer until chiles are soft, about 10 to 15 minutes. Remove from heat. Remove chiles from the water (do not discard) and stem the chiles.

Place the stemmed chiles and 1½ cups of the reserved liquid in a food processor. Process until a smooth paste is formed. Set aside.

Warm the oil in a Dutch oven over medium-high heat. Add in the venison, onion, and garlic. Stir until the venison is browned. Drain any liquid from the Dutch oven. Add in the oregano, cumin, cayenne pepper, chile peppers, tomatoes, and the chile puree. Stir to mix well. Bring to a boil, then reduce heat to let simmer, about 25 minutes. If mixture is too thick (I like chunky chili), then add some of the reserved chile water. During the last 15 minutes, add in the kidney beans and mix well. Season to taste with salt and pepper.

4 dried guajillo chile peppers

4 dried ancho chile peppers

4 cups water

2 tablespoons canola oil

2 pounds ground venison

1 large onion, diced

3 cloves garlic, minced

1 teaspoon dried Mexican oregano

2 teaspoons ground cumin

1 tablespoon ground cayenne pepper

2 canned pickled jalapeno chile peppers, minced

4 medium tomatoes, blanched, peeled, seeded, and chopped

1 can (15 ounces) kidney beans, drained

salt and freshly ground pepper, to taste

Venison Chili Casserole

SERVES: 4 AS A MEAL,
6 AS A SNACK

PREP TIME: 10 MINUTES

COOKING TIME: 20 MINUTES

6 cups chili

2 cups cheddar cheese, shredded (1 and 1)

4 cups white or yellow tortilla chips, crushed

2 cups blue tortilla chips, crushed

1 cup sour cream

½ cup black olives, sliced

¼ cup jalapeno peppers, sliced

This is a recipe that is just as tasty using either chili just made or chili from a day or two before.

Place the chili in an 11-by-17-inch glass baking dish and spread evenly. Top with 1 cup cheese. Alternate strips of yellow and blue crushed tortilla chips, so there are 2 strips of yellow chips and 2 strips of blue chips. Cover with remaining cheese. Bake at 350°F for 20 minutes. Garnish with sour cream, black olives, and jalapeno peppers.

Chili Chilaquiles With Beer

In Mexican households, a popular method to use up day-old homemade tortillas is to fry them until crisp. This recipe uses fried tortillas in a delicious chili casserole.

Preheat oven to 400°F.

In a large skillet over high heat, add enough oil to reach a depth of about 1 inch. While the oil is hot, work in batches and add tortilla wedges. Cook until crisp and golden. Set aside to drain on a paper towel–lined plate.

Spread the fried tortilla wedges in a 9-by-12-inch baking dish. Top with chili. In a food processor, add the tomatoes, beer, eggs, and sour cream. Process until smooth. Season with salt and pepper, to taste.

Pour the mixture over the chili and tortillas. Top with the grated cheeses. Place in the oven until the cheese has melted, about 25 minutes. Serve warm.

SERVES: 6

PREP TIME: 20 MINUTES

COOKING TIME: 25 MINUTES

1 to 2 cups peanut oil

12 corn tortillas, each cut into 6 wedges

2 to 3 cups venison chili

2 ripe tomatoes, seeded and chopped

1 cup beer (Corona will do well)

3 eggs

1 cup sour cream

salt and freshly ground pepper, to taste

1 cup Monterey Jack cheese, grated

1 cup cheddar cheese, grated

Note: If you want to prepare this recipe even more quickly, use white tortilla chips, which are readily available in most food stores.

Great Plains Venison Chili Burritos

SERVES: 4 (2 BURRITOS EACH)
PREP TIME: 10 MINUTES
COOKING TIME: 15 MINUTES

I created this recipe one day when I didn't have time to prepare the traditional meat filling and used leftover chili in its place. To add spice to the burritos, I sautéed some roasted poblano chile pepper strips and added them to the chili mixture.

1 ½ pounds venison chili

1 tablespoon canola oil

1 fresh poblano chile pepper, roasted, peeled, and cut into thin strips

1 cup refried beans

8 flour tortillas, 8 to 10 inches in diameter

1 cup red onions, chopped

1 cup thick salsa (I like Imus or Picante)

1 cup guacamole

In a large saucepan over medium heat, heat up the chili, stirring occasionally. In a small sauté pan, heat the oil over medium-high heat. Add the chile strips and sauté, stirring for about 1 to 2 minutes. Add the chile strips to the chili and mix well.

In a heavy-bottomed saucepan over medium heat, heat the refried beans, adding water if necessary to make a thick sauce. Once the refried beans are heated and the chili is warmed, arrange all the other ingredients in bowls for quick assembly.

In a nonstick frying pan over medium heat, warm the tortillas turning once on each side.

Place some of the chili mixture in the center of each tortilla. Top with some of the refried beans, onions, salsa, and guacamole. Fold in the sides over each other and then fold in the tops. Place each burrito seam-side down on a baking sheet and keep warm in the oven until all burritos are prepared or serve each pair immediately. Garnish with sour cream or grated cheddar cheese on the side.

Mini Chili Cupcakes

This great starter will put everyone's appetite on hold if dinner won't be ready for a while. It is also a great mid-afternoon snack that can easily be prepared when using chili that has already been made.

Preheat oven to 450°F. On a lightly floured work surface, roll out each of the piecrusts to a ⅜-inch thickness. With a pastry cutter, starting at the edge of the dough, cut circles of about 4½ inches in diameter. The piecrusts should yield 8 circles.

Lightly spray oil on the inside of the muffin tins. Place the round dough piece into the muffin cups, lightly pressing edges together where they overlap. Prick the bottom of the dough with a fork a few times to minimize puffing when baked. You can also place a few dried beans or baking beans on the bottom of each cup to help prevent puffing. When all cups are filled, place the muffin tins on a cookie sheet and bake for 8 minutes. Remove from the oven and let cool.

Fill the muffin cups with about 2 tablespoons of the chili and place back in the oven (with the muffin tins on a baking sheet) for about 10 minutes. When there is 1 minute left to bake, sprinkle a little cheddar cheese on each of the chili cupcakes and let bake long enough to let the cheese melt.

Remove from oven and let cool 1 minute on a rack. Carefully remove each chili cupcake and serve.

SERVES: 4
PREP TIME: 15 MINUTES
COOKING TIME: 20 MINUTES

2 piecrusts, 8 ounces each

2 to 3 cups venison chili

2 muffin pans (with 6 muffin holes each)

1 cup cheddar cheese, shredded

Pronto Chili Taco Salad

SERVES: 4 TO 6

PREP TIME: 20 MINUTES

ASSEMBLY TIME: 5 MINUTES

COOKING TIME: 15 MINUTES

1 ½ pounds ripe tomatoes

2 cloves garlic, chopped

1 teaspoon salt

freshly ground black pepper,
    to taste

2 tablespoons canola oil
    (1 and 1)

½ large white onion, chopped

1 pound ground venison

¼ cup kidney beans

1 tablespoon chile powder

½ teaspoon ground cumin

6 cups iceberg or romaine let-
    tuce, shredded

½ cup sliced black olives

1 cup red onion, diced (½ and ½)

1 cup cheddar cheese, shredded

3 cups tortilla chips, broken

When you want to prepare a nutritious and light, yet still satisfying, summer lunch, this recipe is ideal. It's quick to prepare
and yields a beautiful plate presentation. Or, if you want to
make this even faster, heat up some chili and use it instead of the
meat mixture!

Combine the chopped tomatoes, garlic, salt, and pepper in a food
processor. Process until completely combined—about 2 minutes.

Warm 1 tablespoon of the oil in a skillet over medium heat. Add
the tomato mixture and cook about 10 minutes. Set aside to cool.

Warm the other tablespoon of oil in a skillet over medium-high
heat, add in the chopped white onion, and cook until almost
translucent. Add the ground venison. Stir while cooking, until
the meat is browned. Add the kidney beans, chile powder,
ground cumin, and ¼ cup of the tomato sauce. Stir to combine
well. Turn off heat, but let the mixture stay warm in the pan.

In a large salad bowl, combine the lettuce, olives, and ½ cup of
the red onions. Toss to mix well. Create a pocket in the center
of the lettuce mixture and place the warmed venison mix in the
center and top with ½ cup red onions. Around the top of the
salad, sprinkle the grated cheddar cheese and tortilla chips.

Serve at once with the remaining tomato sauce and some
sour cream as an accompaniment.

Don't Leave Me Out

Make sure to refrigerate all leftover
food and sauces. With the high heat
of the grill and outdoor tempera-
tures, it is important to chill any leftover foods as quickly as possible to
reduce any bacterial growth.

Chili Potatoes

I first tried this recipe while on a remote trip in New York's Adirondack Mountains. After a day's outing that left our stomachs aching for dinner—this aptly filled the void.

Preheat the grill for about 20 minutes. The grill should be hot enough that you can hold your hand over it for only a few seconds.

With a fork, poke a few holes in the baking potatoes to allow steam to escape during cooking. Wrap the potatoes twice-around with foil and close tightly. Place the potatoes on the grill and cover. If you will be cooking other food while the potatoes are cooking, place them on the side of the grill. If the potatoes are the only foodstuffs being cooked, then place them on a cooking shelf up off the grill and make sure the internal temperature of the grill, with the lid closed, is about 350° to 375°F.

Let bake about 1 hour—test with a fork to see when done. You should be able to easily insert a fork into the potato when it is thoroughly cooked.

While the potatoes cool slightly, heat up the chili. Slice open the top of the potato and break up the flesh of the potato with a fork. Top with about ¼ cup chili and sprinkle with cheese.

SERVES: 4

PREP TIME: 10 MINUTES

COOKING TIME: 1 HOUR

4 large baking potatoes

1 to 1½ cups venison chili

1 cup cheddar or Monterey Jack cheese, shredded

aluminum foil

South-o'-the-Border Venison & Rice Chili

SERVES: 4

PREP TIME: 10 MINUTES

COOKING TIME: 30 MINUTES

1 pound ground venison

1 package (6.8 ounces)
quick Spanish rice
(with seasoning packet)

3 cups water

1 can (16 ounces) red kidney
beans, rinsed and drained

1 can (15 ounce) kernel corn

1 can (16 ounces) plum tomatoes,
undrained, but broken by hand

1 medium green bell pepper,
chopped

2 teaspoons chile powder

1 teaspoon ground cumin

¾ cup cheddar cheese, shredded

More rice is eaten than any other grain in the world. It comes in short, long, and medium grains—but the long and medium grains are used most often for side dishes. Chili and rice are natural partners, and this recipe is a delicious combination of the two.

In a skillet over medium heat, brown the venison. Set aside.

In a large skillet, combine the rice, seasoning mix, water, beans, corn, tomatoes, green pepper, chile powder, and cumin. Bring to a boil over high heat.

Reduce the heat to low, simmer uncovered for about 10 minutes. Add in the meat and stir to mix thoroughly. Cook an additional 10 minutes or so until the rice is tender.

Portion onto plates and top with grated cheese.

Venison Chili Shepherd's Pie

Here's a recipe that incorporates already-made chili. When I know there will be a lot of meal preparation for friends who will be staying a few days, I usually make a large batch of chili and use the leftovers in a meal such as this one.

SERVES: 6

PREP TIME: 30 MINUTES

COOKING TIME: 1 HOUR

Preheat oven to 425°F.

Boil the potatoes until tender (they should break apart easily when poked with a fork). Drain and reserve about 1 cup of the water. Place the potatoes in a large bowl; add the butter, evaporated milk, salt, and pepper. Beat with an electric mixer until smooth. Use some of the potato water if it becomes too thick. A few small lumps are okay and will add some texture to the potatoes.

In a large skillet over medium-high heat, heat the olive oil and then sauté the carrots and onions about 1 minute. Add the zucchini and yellow squash and the remaining seasonings. Stir frequently about 3 to 5 minutes. Set aside.

In a large, 13-by-9-inch baking pan, spread out the venison chili. Layer the undrained sautéed vegetables on top of the chili, but not too close to the edges. Next, layer the mashed potatoes on top of the vegetables and to the edges. Bake in the oven about 15 to 20 minutes, until the potatoes are browned on top.

1 ½ pounds white potatoes, peeled and cut in quarters

¼ pound unsalted butter (1 stick)

½ cup evaporated milk

1 teaspoon salt

1 teaspoon pepper

1 to 2 tablespoons olive oil

1 cup carrots, diced

1 cup onions, diced

1 cup zucchini, diced

1 cup yellow squash, diced

¼ teaspoon onion powder

¼ teaspoon garlic powder

¼ teaspoon ground cayenne pepper

6 to 8 cups venison chili, room temperature

Chili Strudel

SERVES: 6

PREP TIME: 20 MINUTES

COOKING TIME: 40 MINUTES

12 sheets of phyllo pastry, cool

1 pound prepared venison chili (see Quick-Fix Venison Chili on page 91)

1 cup cheddar cheese, shredded

½ cup unsalted butter, melted

Strudel is the name of a pastry made with a special paper-thin dough. Prepared strudel dough, or phyllo pastry dough, is of good quality and readily available. The combination of this light, flaky crust and savory chili is irresistible.

Preheat oven to 350°F. Butter a baking sheet. To keep the phyllo sheets from drying out, place a damp clean kitchen towel on top of them.

Place a phyllo sheet on the counter with the long side toward you and brush it lightly with butter. Place another sheet on top and brush it with butter also. Repeat until 6 sheets have been used. Place ½ of the chili mixture in a long strip along the edge nearest you, leaving a 1-inch border. Sprinkle with shredded cheese. Fold in the ends and start rolling up the longest edge away from you. Repeat with the remaining phyllo sheets and chili.

Place the 2 phyllo rolls on the buttered baking sheet. Brush with the remaining butter. Bake until golden brown, about 30 to 40 minutes. Cut in ½-inch thick slices and serve warm.

Venison Chili Tostadas

This has also been called "Crispy Chili Pizza" in our household. It's a hit with the younger crowd!

SERVES: 6

PREP TIME: 10 MINUTES

COOKING TIME: 15 MINUTES

In a small sauté pan over high heat, add canola oil to a depth of about ½ inch. When the oil is very hot, add the tortillas, one at a time and fry until crisp and golden. Remove and drain on paper towels.

In a small sauté pan over low heat, reheat the chili. Prepare 2 tortillas per person. Spread out the chili on each tortilla. Top with a layer of lettuce, onion, and tomato. Season with salt. Top each one with small dollops of sour cream and sliced olives. Serve immediately.

1 to 2 cups canola oil

12 corn tortillas, 6 inches in diameter

¾ pound prepared venison chili (see Quick-Fix Venison Chili on page 91)

3 cups lettuce, shredded

1 red onion, thinly sliced

4 ripe plum tomatoes, thinly sliced

salt, to taste

1 cup sour cream

1/4 cup black olives, sliced

Venison Chili Quesadillas

SERVES: 6

PREP TIME: 5 MINUTES

COOKING TIME: 30 MINUTES

canola oil, as needed

12 tortillas, 6 inches in diameter

4 cups prepared venison chili, room temperature

3 cups cheddar cheese, shredded

2 fresh Serrano chile peppers, finely chopped and seeds removed

2 cups Sizzlin' Fresh Tomato Salsa (see page 138)

Serrano chiles are hotter, smaller, and thinner than jalapeno chiles. Be careful when handling them. If your skin is sensitive, wear plastic gloves. If your guests don't like the heat of Serrano chiles, prepare a few quesadillas with the milder California chile.

In a large skillet over medium heat, heat ½ teaspoon canola oil. When hot, place 1 tortilla in the skillet. Place some chili atop half of the tortilla, leaving a ½-inch border. Sprinkle some of the cheese and a little of the chile peppers on top of the chili. Fold the uncovered portion of the tortilla over the filling and press the edges together. Flip the tortilla and cook on the other side, adding a small amount of oil, if necessary. Remove and keep warm.

Repeat with the remaining tortillas. Serve with salsa.

Chili Stuffed Green Peppers

This is a twist on the classic stuffed green peppers. Ready-made venison chili comes in handy when preparing this scrumptious recipe.

SERVES: 6

PREP TIME: 5 MINUTES

COOKING TIME: 45 MINUTES

Preheat oven to 350°F.

Remove the tops of the peppers and seed. Parboil the peppers in a pot of boiling water for about 3 to 5 minutes. Drain and rinse with cool water to stop the cooking.

Divide mixture into 6 parts and fill each pepper. Pour tomato sauce on the bottom of a 13-by-9-by-2-inch glass baking dish. Place the stuffed peppers in the glass baking dish and bake for about 40 minutes. During the last 10 minutes, top the peppers with cheese.

6 large green bell peppers

1 pound venison chili (see Quick-Fix Venison Chili on page 91)

2 cups tomato sauce

½ pound cheddar cheese, grated

CHAPTER THREE

Venison Accompaniments

Here are some of my own favorite side dishes that work well with venison. Many of them are for the grill.

Just think, your entire meal can be prepared outdoors and away from the kitchen. You can heat up some Crunchy Grilled Garlic Bread, Grilled Potatoes, and Garlic Grilled Mushrooms to accompany some grilled Zesty Elk Steaks—and never have to heat up a kitchen appliance!

Grilled Mushrooms & Onions

SERVES: 4

PREP TIME: 10 MINUTES

COOKING TIME: 10 TO 15 MINUTES

¾ pound mushrooms, washed and sliced

2 onions, peeled and sliced

4 garlic cloves, peeled and crushed

8 tablespoons unsalted butter

salt and pepper, to taste

heavy-duty aluminum foil for 4 double-layered packets

Preheat the grill for about 20 minutes. The grill should be hot enough that you can hold your hand over it for only a few seconds.

Divide the mushrooms and onions into 4 portions and place each on a double layer of heavy-duty aluminum foil. Place 1 crushed garlic clove on top of each parcel. Dot each with 2 tablespoons of butter. Season with salt and freshly ground pepper. Wrap the packages in butcher-wrap style, leaving an air pocket at the top.

Place the packages on the grill and let cook about 10 to 15 minutes. Lift and shake slightly to toss the mushrooms and onions from time to time.

Remove from grill and serve warm.

Grilling Veggies

Great vegetables to grill include bell peppers: They can be roasted on the grill and then tossed with pasta.

Cheesy Grilled Zucchini

Preheat the grill for about 20 minutes. The grill should be hot enough that you can hold your hand over it for only a few seconds.

Place the zucchini slices in a flat-bottomed glass dish and pour the Italian dressing over them. Turn the slices to coat evenly.

Place the slices in a hinged grilling basket. Place over the grills and turn every 3 or 4 minutes. When they are just cooked through, sprinkle with the no-salt Italian seasoning and the Parmesan cheese and cook about 3 to 5 minutes longer. Serve warm.

SERVES: 4

PREP TIME: 10 MINUTES

COOKING TIME: 10 MINUTES

4 medium zucchinis, sliced lengthwise about ¼ inch thick

¼ cup Italian dressing

4 teaspoons no-salt Italian seasoning (I like Mrs. Dash's Classic Italiano)

¼ cup Parmesan cheese, grated

Grilled Portobello Mushroom Salad

SERVES 4

PREP TIME: 15 MINUTES

COOKING TIME: 10 MINUTES

4 large fresh portobello mushrooms, cleaned and with stems removed

1¼ cup Italian dressing made with red wine vinegar

6 cups assorted salad greens

4 small tomatoes, sliced in quarters

freshly ground pepper, to taste

Place the mushroom caps in a flat-bottomed, glass baking dish. Pour 1 cup of the dressing over the mushrooms and turn to coat the mushrooms thoroughly. Marinate at room temperature for about 1 hour, turning occasionally.

Preheat the grill for about 20 minutes. The grill should be hot enough that you can hold your hand over it for only a few seconds.

Place the mushrooms on the grill and cover. Grill about 4 minutes on each side. When done, remove from the grill and let sit about 1 minute. Slice each cap into ¼-inch slices.

Pour the reserved dressing onto the salad greens and toss to coat well. Divide the salad greens onto 4 plates. Layer the mushroom caps on top of the salad and place the tomato quarters around the mushrooms. Season with freshly ground pepper and serve.

Balsamic Grilled Red Onions

Place the sliced onions in a shallow, flat glass dish. Combine the remaining ingredients in a small bowl. Stir to mix well. Pour over the onions. Let them sit for about 30 minutes.

Preheat the grill for about 10 minutes. It should be at a medium-hot setting—not as high as you would normally prepare it for grilling meats. You will be able to hold your hand over it for several seconds.

Place the onion slices in a hinged grill basket. Grill them for about 15 to 20 minutes, depending upon the heat of the grill. Turn the onions every few minutes. They are done when browned slightly on both sides. Serve warm.

SERVES: 4

PREP TIME: 10 MINUTES

MARINATING TIME: 30 MINUTES

COOKING TIME: 20 MINUTES

2 large red onions, peeled, sliced in ½-inch thick slices

1 tablespoon soy sauce

3 tablespoons balsamic vinegar

1 tablespoon canola oil

1 teaspoon Dijon-style mustard

Grilled Eggplant & Smoked Mozzarella

SERVES: 4

PREP TIME: 10 MINUTES

COOKING TIME: 15 MINUTES

1 large eggplant,
  about 6 inches long

¼ cup salt

½ cup oil and balsamic vinegar
  dressing

10 to 12 slices smoked
  mozzarella cheese

Preheat the grill for about 20 minutes. The grill should be hot enough that you can hold your hand over it for only a few seconds.

Cut the eggplant into slices that are about ½ inch thick. Place the slices either in a colander or over a few cookie cooling racks on top of cookie sheets. Sprinkle salt over the eggplant slices on both sides to draw out the moisture. Let them stand for about 30 minutes.

Blot the eggplant slices dry with paper towels. Brush one side of the eggplant slices with the balsamic dressing and place this side of the eggplant on the grill. Brush the other side of the eggplant slices with the dressing while they are grilling. Let them grill about 5 minutes each side.

A few minutes before the eggplant is done, place a slice of smoked mozzarella cheese on top of each eggplant slice and cover the grill for about 1 to 2 minutes. Remove from the grill when the cheese has melted. Serve warm.

Give Them Room!

Don't overcrowd a grill. If food is packed too closely it may steam instead of searing over the high heat. If you have a lot of items to cook, first sear the food that will cook the longest and then place it either on an elevated grill rack or on a cooler part of the grill to continue cooking while other food is cooked in the hotter sections.

Crunchy Grilled Garlic Bread

Preheat the grill for about 20 minutes. The grill should be hot enough that you can hold your hand over it for only a few seconds. You will be cooking the bread on a rack elevated above the main cooking grill.

In a sauté pan, melt the butter over medium heat. Add in the minced garlic and stir for about 5 minutes. Do not let the garlic brown. Remove from heat and stir in the dried oregano.

Place the bread on a large piece of aluminum foil. Cut the bread on a diagonal into 1-inch slices. Do not cut all the way through the bottom. Pry open each slice and spoon in some of the melted garlic butter mixture. If there is any leftover butter, drizzle it across the top of the bread. Fold up and seal the bread in the foil.

Place the bread on a rack above the grill. Close the grill and heat for about 10 minutes. If the grill is left open, heat for about 15 minutes. Once the bread is heated through, remove it from the foil and place it directly on the grill, upside down, for about 10 to 15 seconds to crisp the very top of the bread. Remove from the grill and serve piping hot.

SERVES: 4 TO 6
PREP TIME: 10 MINUTES
COOKING TIME: 12 MINUTES

6 tablespoons unsalted butter
4 cloves garlic, minced
½ teaspoon dried oregano
1 large French baguette

Sizzlin' Fresh Tomato Salsa

YIELD: 4 CUPS

PREP TIME: 15 MINUTES

COOKING TIME: 5 MINUTES

2½ pounds fresh tomatoes

1 large red onion, peeled and quartered

1 fresh jalapeno pepper

4 Serrano chiles, minced

⅓ cup fresh cilantro, chopped

1 tablespoon garlic, minced

2 limes

1 bunch scallions (green onions), white parts chopped

hot red pepper sauce, to taste

salt and black pepper, to taste

Blanch the tomatoes in a pot of boiling water for about 20 seconds. Transfer to a bowl filled with ice and water to cool. Peel, seed, and chop.

Place the tomatoes, onion, jalapeno peppers, Serrano chiles, cilantro, garlic, juice from the 2 limes, and scallions in a blender. Blend for about 30 seconds to 1 minute. Season with hot sauce and salt and pepper. Chill for about 1 hour; serve at room temperature.

Grilled Husky Corn

Preheat the grill for about 20 minutes. The grill should be warm enough that you can hold your hand over it for several seconds, but no more.

Soak the unhusked corn in cold water for 30 minutes. Peel back the husks without pulling them all the way off. Pull out the silk. Spread about 1 tablespoon of butter on the corn. Fold back the husks around the corn and twist the tops to close. Place the corn on the grill and cook until tender, about 15 minutes. Turn occasionally.

SERVES: 6

PREP TIME: 40 MINUTES

COOKING TIME: 15 MINUTES

6 ears of corn in husks

½ cup butter, room temperature

Grilled Potatoes

SERVES: 4

PREP TIME: 15 MINUTES

COOKING TIME: 20 MINUTES

4 large baking potatoes,
scrubbed, skin on

½ cup unsalted butter

2 cloves garlic, minced

1 tablespoon dried rosemary

¼ cup grated Parmesan cheese

4 pieces of double-layered foil

Slice baking potatoes in ½-inch thick slices. Prepare the 4 pieces of double-layered foil to wrap the slices in—1 for each person.

Melt 2 tablespoons of butter and divide equally among the 4 pieces of foil. Fan the slices of potatoes, 1 potato per foil wrap. Top each potato with minced garlic, rosemary, and Parmesan cheese and dot with the remaining butter.

Seal the foil packets and set on grill. Cook until tender, about 15 to 20 minutes. Serve hot. Be careful of any escaping steam when opening the packets.

Corn 'n' Pepper Summer Salad

Mix the corn, peppers, scallions, olives, parsley, olive oil, lime juice, and cumin in a large bowl. Season with salt and pepper. Portion into individual bowls or as a side dish with burgers or steaks.

SERVES: 4

PREP TIME: 20 MINUTES

2 packages (10 ounces) frozen whole kernel corn, cooked, drained, and cooled

1 red bell pepper, diced

1 orange bell pepper, diced

3 scallions (green onions), diced

½ cup black olives, chopped

2 tablespoons parsley, minced

¼ cup olive oil

1 tablespoon fresh lime juice

½ teaspoon ground cumin

salt and freshly ground pepper, to taste

CHAPTER FOUR

Marinades, Butters, Rubs, and Sauces

I love the taste of venison. Yet, many people try to mask venison's flavor with a marinade or sauce. That isn't always necessary. Sure, occasionally there is a piece of meat that was not properly cared for in the field or came from a very old animal and needs a little help in masking its gamy taste. But, for the most part, venison is simply delicious seasoned with just a bit of salt and pepper.

With that said, the following recipes for marinades, rubs, butters, and sauces are meant to complement venison—not overpower it. After all, good seasoning doesn't hurt any piece of meat.

Marinades

Venison has a unique and delicious taste of its own, and I like to use marinades to simply add a new flavor to it. Since most marinades soften meat, I suggest marinating tender cuts of venison, such as a loin steak or cutlet, for no longer than an hour or so. The meat will take on the new flavor, yet not lose its texture.

A marinade often contains some type of acidic ingredient, such as wine, lemon juice, or vinegar, to improve the texture of the meat. Also included in the marinade is some type of oil to offer a moisture-based coating for cooking. Some oils are neutral in flavor, such as sunflower and canola, and other oils impart their flavor, as do extra virgin olive oil and sesame oil. Other ingredients that impart their flavor to the meat include garlic, spices, and herbs. These ingredients must be balanced so as not to overpower the marinade. To get the most flavor from any of the aromatic members of the lily family—garlic, shallots, scallions and onions—chop them as finely as possible.

Larger, thicker cuts of meat should be marinated longer than smaller cuts. For example, I might marinate a large chuck roast overnight, but only marinate a small venison steak an hour or two.

Marinades should be prepared in a nonreactive container, made of plastic, ceramic, or glass. (A large zip-lock plastic bag will even do.) An aluminum or iron container may react with the acid in the marinade and infuse it with a metallic taste. Meat should also be marinated in the refrigerator. Ideally, the meat should be covered completely with the marinade. If you are going to marinate a steak for a short period of time, you can use less liquid, but the steak should be turned from time to time to ensure uniform penetration.

Tip: If you marinate a piece of venison and want to use the marinade as a baste while it's on the grill, always boil it for about three to five minutes first. Bacteria may have multiplied in the marinade while the meat was marinating. If it isn't boiled to kill the bacteria, you could just be reintroducing the bacteria back into the meat.

Smoky Marinade

¾ cup liquid smoke (such as Stubb's Mesquite Liquid Smoke)

1 cup Worcestershire sauce

1 cup soy sauce

½ cup lemon juice

½ cup orange juice

½ cup brown sugar

¼ cup canola oil

2 tablespoons freshly ground black pepper

½ teaspoon cayenne pepper

2 garlic cloves, minced

Combine all the ingredients and let sit for about 1 hour for the flavors to blend.

Can be used as a marinade for venison steaks, up to 1 or 2 hours depending upon the thickness of the steaks.

Oriental Marinade

¾ cup soy sauce

¾ cup mirin (rice wine)

1 teaspoon fresh ginger, minced

1 teaspoon sugar

1 clove garlic, minced

Combine all ingredients in a nonreactive container. Use as a marinade for steaks or loin cuts.

Dijon Mustard Marinade

In a small non-reactive bowl, combine all the ingredients. Mix well. Use as a marinade for steaks or loin cuts.

1 cup canola oil

⅓ cup Dijon-style mustard

⅓ cup rice wine vinegar

1 tablespoon fresh lemon juice

freshly ground pepper, to taste

Zesty Molasses Marinade

Mix all ingredients together and let sit for 1 hour for the flavors to blend.

Great for whole tenderloins.

1 cup molasses

1 tablespoon balsamic vinegar

1 tablespoon lemon juice

2 tablespoons freshly ground black pepper

3 garlic cloves, minced

1 tablespoon dry mustard

2 teaspoons fresh ginger, grated

1 teaspoon dried thyme

½ teaspoon dried red pepper flakes

Butters

A compound butter is made by softening butter and then mixing in various ingredients. The mixture is then rolled into a cylinder and chilled. Most of the butters in this book call for slicing the chilled butter and placing a dab on a sizzling piece of venison, hot off the grill. Compound butters offer a simple way to add luxurious flavor to your meals.

Shallot-Lemon Butter

1 ½ tablespoons shallots, minced

1 teaspoon dry white wine

1 teaspoons lemon zest, minced

¼ teaspoon freshly ground white pepper (you can use black pepper, but it will be more evident in the butter than the white pepper)

salt, to taste

¼ cup unsalted butter, room temperature

Combine the shallots, white wine, lemon zest, salt, and pepper in a small bowl. Mix with a fork to combine thoroughly. Add in the butter, a piece at a time, and mix well.

Place in a small serving bowl and serve at room temperature or chill. If you want to chill it, place the butter on some wax paper or foil, shape into a 1-inch log and place in the freezer for 45 minutes.

I like to use this while they are cooking on venison steaks and even use a dollop after they are pulled off the grill, while still hot.

Chile Butter

¼ cup unsalted butter, room
temperature

2 tablespoons chile powder

1 teaspoon ground cumin

In a small bowl, mix the butter and the spices with a fork. Mix well until all spices are thoroughly combined. Place in a small serving bowl and serve at room temperature or chill. If you want to chill it, place the butter on some wax paper or foil, shape into a 1-inch log and place in the freezer for 45 minutes.

I like to use this on venison hamburgers as well as on grilled vegetables.

Blue Cheese Butter

½ cup unsalted whipped butter,
softened

5 tablespoons blue cheese,
crumbled

2 shallots, minced

salt and pepper to taste

While this recipe calls for whipped butter (I find it much easier to work with when making seasoned butters), regular unsalted butter will work also. Just make sure it is at room temperature before mixing.

In a small, bowl, mix the butter, blue cheese, and shallots well with a fork. Season with salt and pepper to taste. Dollop the mixture onto a piece of plastic wrap and roll it into a small log shape, using the plastic wrap. Refrigerate the wrapped log for a few hours or freeze for 20 minutes. When the butter is set, slice it in ¼-inch slices and place on top of burgers or steaks.

Garlic Butter

In a small saucepan, heat one-half tablespoon butter over low heat. Add the minced garlic and cook until soft. Do not let the garlic burn, or it will taste bitter.

Place the stick of butter in a small bowl and mash with a fork. Add the cooked garlic, salt and continue to blend with the fork until thoroughly combined.

Dollop the mixture onto a piece of plastic wrap and roll it into a small log shape, using the plastic wrap. Refrigerate the wrapped log for a few hours or freeze for 20 minutes. When the butter is set, slice it in ¼-inch slices and place on top of burgers or steaks.

1 stick (8 tablespoons) plus one-half tablespoons unsalted butter, room temperature

4 large garlic cloves, minced

1 teaspoon kosher or sea salt

Rubs

Rubs are blends of herbs, spices, salt, and pepper. These rubs sit on the surface of the meat and impart their flavor through the surface. If they are grilled, these rubs form a flavorful crust. They are simple to make and can be made in batches to save for future use.

There is nothing like the powerful flavor of freshly ground spices. For example, if a recipe calls for ground pepper, use whole peppercorns and grind them with a peppermill. The pre-ground pepper readily available in the grocery store has a mild taste and loses its flavor quickly. Fresh, whole spices will make a difference in preparing rubs.

If you prepare a large portion of a rub and do not use it all, store it in an opaque container in the refrigerator. Both light and heat will quickly ruin a good rub. While storage times vary, a dry rub will last about two to three months in the refrigerator. After that period, you can add it to some breading mixture, soup, or even hamburger meat and toss the rest away.

Tri-Color Lemon Pepper Rub

1 tablespoon sea salt

2 tablespoons minced lemon zest

⅓ cup freshly ground peppercorns (black, pink, and white)

Place all ingredients in a mortar and grind slightly to combine. Use as a rub for venison steak or cutlets.

Garlic-Lime Rub

In a mortar, combine the salt, pepper, garlic, cumin and ground cayenne pepper. Grind the ingredients to a paste. Slowly drizzle in the lime juice and olive oil, alternately, until it has reached a smooth consistency. This is a moist rub and should be used the same day as it is prepared.

1 teaspoon kosher salt

½ teaspoon freshly ground black pepper

6 cloves garlic, minced

½ teaspoon cumin

⅛ teaspoon ground cayenne pepper

½ cup fresh lime juice

2 tablespoons olive oil

Spicy Loin Steak Rub

Mix all ingredients in a small bowl. Use as a rub for loin steaks and wrap the meat in plastic to avoid any additional moisture loss.

1 teaspoon freshly ground pepper

1 teaspoon sea or kosher salt

½ teaspoon cayenne pepper

½ teaspoon ground cloves

1 tablespoon paprika

2 teaspoons garlic, minced

1 teaspoon packed brown sugar

"Aye—There's the Rub" Rub

¼ cup brown sugar

¼ cup paprika

¼ cup chile powder

¼ cup black pepper

1 tablespoon dry mustard

3 tablespoon garlic powder

1 tablespoon sea salt

Mix all the ingredients in a bowl and cover. This is a dry rub that works well with thicker cuts of venison.

Crazy Cajun Seasoning

¼ teaspoon ground cayenne pepper

2 tablespoons ground black pepper

1 tablespoon chile powder

1 tablespoon ground cumin

⅓ cup paprika

2 tablespoons sea salt

Place all the seasonings in a zip-lock plastic bag, seal, and shake thoroughly to combine the seasonings.

Sauces

Sauces are created and used to flatter the food they are served with and not to mask them. With all ingredients in balance, sauces should carry their own unique, well-defined flavor. The brown sauce in this section is meant to complement Venison Wellington but enhances other types of grilled venison, too.

Brown (Is Down) Sauce

In a skillet over medium heat, sauté the onion, celery, carrot, and shallots in the butter until the onion is translucent, about 5 minutes. In a small cup, mix the cornstarch with about ½ cup of the bouillon. Mix until smooth and there are no lumps. Add all the remaining ingredients and the corn starch mixture to the pan and bring to a boil. Reduce the heat and simmer for 20 to 30 minutes. Strain the sauce before serving.

Ideal for Venison Wellington and grilled steaks.

Note: This can be made ahead of time and the sauce can be kept warm. It can also be strained and refrigerated if prepared a day ahead of time.

YIELD: 3 CUPS
PREP TIME: 10 MINUTES
COOKING TIME: 30 MINUTES

4 tablespoons butter

1 small onion, diced

1 small celery stalk, diced

1 carrot, chopped

2 shallots, crushed

3 tablespoons corn starch

3 cups low-salt beef bouillon

2 tablespoons red wine

½ teaspoon ground thyme

1 teaspoon freshly ground black pepper

High-Caliber Mayonnaise

Combine all ingredients in a small bowl. Use immediately or store in the refrigerator.

Excellent accompaniment for grilled venison burgers.

1 cup mayonnaise (such as Hellmann's)

¼ teaspoon garlic, minced

1 teaspoon dried thyme leaves

1 teaspoon fresh chives, minced

hot pepper sauce, to taste

Resources

**MAIL ORDER SOURCES FOR GRILLS
AND ACCESSORIES**

Barr Brothers Company

1540-B Charles Drive
Redding, CA 96003
800-630-8665
www.bbq-tools.com
info@bbq-tools.com
*Forks, skewers, wood chips, brushes,
thermometers, spatulas, tongs, spits,
and more.*

Char-Broil

P.O. Box 1240
Columbus, GA 31902
800-241-7548
*Grills, accessories, vegetable grates, smoker
boxes, and more.*

Coleman Company

3600 North Hydraulic
Wichita, KS 67219
800-835-3278
www.coleman.com
consumerservice@coleman.com
*Charcoal grills, gas grills, grill accessories,
portable grills, and RoadTrip grills.*

EdgeCraft Corp.

Chef's Choice
825 Southwood Road
Avondale, PA 19311
800-341-3255
www.edgecraft.com
*Knife sharpeners, cutlery, electric slicers,
electric kettles, and more.*

The Holland Company, Inc.

600 Irving Parkway
Hollysprings, NC 27540
800-880-9766
www.hollandgrill.com
*All types of grills and grilling accessories:
rib racks, thermometers, tongs, and grill
cleaners.*

Viking

c/o Sohns Appliance Center
23-27 Main Street
Walden, NY 12586
800-473-0508
www.sohns.homeappliances.com
www.vikingrange.com
*High-end gas grills, barbecue tool sets,
portable cast aluminum griddles, and grilling
thermometers.*

Williams-Sonoma

3259 Van Ness Avenue
San Francisco, CA 94109
800-541-2233
*High-end grills and accessories, exotic woods
and chips, condiments, and more.*

MAIL-ORDER AND ON-LINE SOURCES
FOR VENISON AND OTHER FOOD STUFFS

Broadleaf Venison USA, Inc.

5600 South Alameda Street, Suite 100
Vernon, CA 90058
800-336-3844
www.broadleafgame.com
info@broadleafgame.com
*Venison, buffalo, elk, and other wild game
meats and birds.*

Broken Arrow Ranch

104 Highway 27 W
Ingram, TX 78025
800-962-4263
www.brokenarrowranch.com
*Venison, game sausages, chilies, and other
wild game meats.*

Bueno Mexican Foods

P.O. Box 293
Albuquerque, NM 87103
800-95-CHILE
www.buenofoods.com
feedback@buenofoods.com
*Flame-roasted fresh frozen green chiles, red
chiles, salsas and sauces, tortillas, dried chile
pods and chile powders, tamales, enchiladas,
and more.*

D'Artagnan, Inc.

280 Wilson Avenue
Newark, NJ 07105
800-327-8246
www.dartagnan.com
info@dartagnan.com
*Venison, buffalo, and other wild game meats
and birds.*

Durham Meat Company

P.O. Box 390A
Santa Clara, CA 95052
800-233-8742
*Venison, buffalo, caribou, wild game sausages,
and other wild game meats and birds.*

. . . .

The Game Exchange (Polarica)
P.O. Box 880204
San Francisco, CA 94188-0204
800-GAME-USA
www.polarica.com
*Venison, caribou, elk, buffalo, game sausages,
and other wild game meats and birds.*

Game Sales International
P.O. Box 7719
Loveland, CO 80537
800-729-2090
www.gamesalesintl.com
*Venison, buffalo, caribou, elk, and other wild
game meats and birds.*

Hills Foods Ltd.
Unit 130 Glacier Street
Coquitlan, BC
Canada, V3K 5Z6
604-472-1500
www.hillsfoods.com
Note: Wholesale distributors only
*Venison, elk, caribou, bison, and other wild
game meats and birds.*

Jane Butel's Pecos Valley Spice Co.
P.O. Box 964
Albuquerque, NM 87103
800-473-TACO
www.pecosvalley.com
*Ground, crushed and frozen chiles, corn
masa, barbeque mixes and rubs, southwestern
spices, and more.*

Musicon Farms
385 Scotchtown Road
Goshen, NY 10924
845-294-6378
www.koshervenison.com
norman@koshervenison.com
Glatt kosher venison.

Myron's Fine Foods, Inc.
217 East Main Street
Orange, MA 01364
978-544-2820
www.chefmyrons.com
myrons@valinet.com
*Authentic cooking sauces with an Asian flair
for meat, vegetables, seafood, and chicken.*

. . . .

Nicky USA, Inc.
223 Southeast Third Avenue
Portland, OR 97214
800-469-4162
www.nickyusawildgame.com
Venison, elk, bison, caribou, sausages and
other wild game meats and birds.

Prairie Harvest
P.O. Box 1013
Spearfish, SD 57783
800-350-7166
www.prairieharvest.com
Venison, bison, caribou, elk, sausages and
other wild game meats and birds.

The Sausage Maker Inc.
1500 Clinton Street, Building 123
Buffalo, NY 14206
888-490-8525
www.sausagemaker.com
Everything you need to make your own
sausage and then some!

Shaffer Venison Farms, Inc.
RR 1 Box 172
Herndon, PA 17830
800-446-3745
www.shafferfarms.com
shafrfam@ruralife.net
Venison.

Specialty World Foods
84 Montgomery Street
Albany, NY 12207
800-233-0193
Venison, bison, caribou, elk, sausage and
other wild game meats and birds.

Tatonka Buffalo Ranch
3336 State Highway Y
Galena, MO 65656
800-365-2115
www.tatonkabuffalo.com
Buffalo and elk.

Totally Wild Seasonings
10344 CO Rd X-61
Wapello, IA 52653
319-523-4428
www.totallywildseasonings.com
Fish and wild game breading, jerky seasonings,
smoking cures, fried turkey seasonings, and more.

Conversion Charts

LIQUID CONVERSIONS

US	IMPERIAL	METRIC
2 tbs	1 fl oz	30 ml
3 tbs	1½ fl oz	45 ml
¼ cup	2 fl oz	60 ml
⅓ cup	2½ fl oz	75 ml
½ cup	4 fl oz	125 ml
⅔ cup	5 fl oz	150 ml
¾ cup	6 fl oz	175 ml
1 cup	8 fl oz	250 ml
1¼ cups	10 fl oz	300 ml
1⅓ cups	11 fl oz	325 ml
1½ cups	12 fl oz	350 ml
1⅔ cups	13 fl oz	375 ml
1¾ cups	14 fl oz	400 ml
2 cups (1 pint)	16 fl oz	500 ml
2 pints	1¾ pints	1 liter

WEIGHT CONVERSIONS

US/UK	METRIC
½ oz	15 g
1 oz	30 g
1½ oz	45 g
2 oz	60 g
2½ oz	70 g
3 oz	85 g
3½ oz	100 g
4 oz	115 g
5 oz	140 g
6 oz	175 g
7 oz	200 g
8 oz	225 g
9 oz	250 g
10 oz	300 g
11 oz	325 g
12 oz	350 g
13 oz	375 g
14 oz	400 g
15 oz	425 g
1 lb	450 g

OVEN TEMPERATURES

FAHRENHEIT	CELSIUS
250°	120°
275°	140°
300°	150°
325°	160°
350°	180°
375°	190°
400°	200°
425°	220°
450°	230°
475°	240°
500°	260°

Index

...